Metrics
That
Matter

Counting
WHAT'S REALLY IMPORTANT
to
COLLEGE STUDENTS

Metrics
That
Matter

**Zachary Bleemer, Mukul Kumar,
Aashish Mehta, Chris Muellerleile,
and Christopher Newfield**

Johns Hopkins University Press

BALTIMORE

Johns Hopkins University Press
2715 North Charles Street
Baltimore, Maryland 21218
www.press.jhu.edu

Library of Congress Cataloging-in-Publication Data

Names: Bleemer, Zachary, 1991– author. | Kumar, Mukul, 1984– author. |
    Mehta, Aashish, 1974– author. | Muellerleile, Christopher, author. | Newfield,
    Christopher, author.
Title: Metrics that matter : counting what's really important to college students /
    Zachary Bleemer, Mukul Kumar, Aashish Mehta, Christopher Muellerleile, and
    Christopher Newfield.
Description: Baltimore : Johns Hopkins University Press, 2023. | Includes
    bibliographical references and index.
Identifiers: LCCN 2022024591 | ISBN 9781421445731 (paperback) |
    ISBN 9781421445748 (ebook)
Subjects: LCSH: Universities and colleges—United States—Evaluation. | Universities
    and colleges—Ratings and rankings—United States. | Universities and colleges—
    United States—Admission. | College costs—United States. | Student loans—
    United States. | College graduates—United States—Finance, Personal. |
    College majors—United States. | Educational indicators—United States.
Classification: LCC LB2331.62 .B54 2023 | DDC 378—dc23/eng/20220719
LC record available at https://lccn.loc.gov/2022024591

A catalog record for this book is available from the British Library.

Special discounts are available for bulk purchases of this book.
For more information, please contact Special Sales at specialsales@jh.edu.

Contents

Preface

High school and college students are surrounded by a proliferation of indicators and rankings that purport to help them decide where to go to college and what to study once they're there. This book takes a critical look at the most popular of these metrics. Chapters focus on colleges' "return on investment," university rankings, average student debt, average wages by college major, and more. Writing mainly for students and their families, we explain the ways each of these metrics is flawed—and in some cases fundamentally misleading—as a basis for making important educational decisions. We also delineate the ways that students' reliance on certain metrics have skewed universities' incentives away from high-quality education and distorted students' and the broader public's perceptions of the end goal of higher education, overemphasizing private financial returns over its broad economic and social benefits.

Drawing on decades of scholarship from the economics of education, social theory, university studies, and other disciplines, we pair each metric with a concrete recommendation for additional information, both qualitative and quantitative, or alternative perspectives that would be more useful for students to consider. For example, instead of measuring the quality of universities by their selectivity, students would be better served by focusing on how much money universities annually invest in educating each of their students. Students should pay no attention to universities' posted tuition prices and can instead turn to innovative net price calculators such as MyinTuition to get a sense of what attending college would actually cost them. While "social mobility rankings" have recently received substantial media attention, better information than these popular metrics is available to today's students and the wider public. Lower-income students should also scrutinize student stratification across universities' fields of study and whether universities restrict access to their most popular majors. This book aims to facilitate important educational decisions while simultaneously reorienting public perceptions of the manifold values of higher education.

Metrics
That
Matter

Introduction

The college admissions scandal that emerged in 2019 from the FBI's Operation Varsity Blues was the biggest college news story in years.[1] It had everything a story could ask for: famous universities, obnoxious cheating, celebrity villains, and public shaming, all seeming to confirm the widespread belief that college admissions is corrupt.

Years later, the scandal has not been forgotten. But as cynics predicted, almost nothing has changed. The desperate scramble to get students into increasingly and even ridiculously selective colleges continues. Fewer than a handful of universities have ended their long-standing practices of tilting their admissions scales toward big donors and the children of their alumni. Even if a few side doors to admission have been slammed shut, the scandal didn't make selective college admissions generally more equitable and it didn't make colleges better for their students.[2]

Now is a good time to look at some of the deeper factors that have made getting into college such a rat race. One is the sense that a college degree doesn't offer a smooth path to a good job but instead amounts merely to an entry point into a lottery that many people will lose. Anxiety about getting a job and the future of work has fueled the boom in applications to name-brand colleges, which in turn has kept rejection rates sky high and further fueled the next cohort's anxiety about college. In response to the COVID-19 pandemic, many universities stopped requiring applicants to submit standardized test scores with their applications, yet relief from the infamous SAT metric flooded highly selective universities with additional applications and made their admission rates even worse.

Another issue is the fact that state governments have decreased their support for public colleges and universities. The number of seats at good colleges in many states has not increased at the same rate as the growth in the number of qualified high school graduates, and public institutions have struggled to maintain educational quality as their public support has dried up. Many books have been written about the challenges universities face as they work to provide an education that helps their students successfully transition into adulthood.

In this book, we examine a deep issue that has been generally overlooked in this literature: the role of metrics in shaping both the public's understanding of college and the way individual students approach higher education. By *metrics* we mean the numbers used to summarize the features or quality of a college or university. A metric is often expressed as an *indicator*, which measures a specific feature of an institution to allow instant comparison between colleges. One common indicator is a college's stated annual tuition price. Another is the college's graduation rate. Metrics used in these types of comparisons are routinely organized into rankings. The *U.S. News & World Report*'s college rankings, for instance, rely on a formula that uses a variety of indicators such as graduation rates and class size and assembles them into a list of the "best" colleges.

College metrics, indicators, and rankings exist to help people decide whether they should go to college, what college to go to, and what they should study in college. Today, these deliberations are shaped at every step by the kinds of numbers we analyze in the following chapters. We have written this book to show that many of the most common metrics, ratings, rankings, and indicators have distorted many peoples' understanding of college and have misled students and their families. The best-known metrics range from inadequate to misleading. This isn't just true of a couple of popular rankings. Nearly all of the leading university metrics are seriously flawed in some important way. None of the metrics we discuss in the coming chapters should be used as they are currently being used.

The goal of this book is to walk anyone thinking about college through the most common metrics people use to make important decisions about their future. We have written it so that anybody interested in higher education—students, parents, voters, professors, high school guidance counselors—can get control over the numbers. We hope this will help you avoid the mistakes that the available metrics currently encourage.

The five authors of this book have pooled our diverse expertise to explore and expose these metrics. We are professors and researchers in a variety of humanities and social science fields. We have studied the metrics in this book carefully, both individually and as a group. Our goal is to reform the use of metrics by helping people understand how they work, which ones to avoid, which to use, what else to demand, and when not to use a metric at all. We hope to encourage students to match their highly personal and individual college-related goals, needs, and backgrounds to specific institutions and fields of study by collecting comprehensive information about their choices. We also want to expand students' and their families' understanding of what a college degree is supposed to do, both for themselves and for society.

We have organized the book in the order that aspiring students and their family, friends, neighbors, counselors, and teachers encounter the metrics that shape their thinking about the high-stakes decisions people make when considering a college education. The sections do not need to be read in this order. Each chapter is a self-contained discussion of a single metric that explains where the numbers come from and how well they would serve you (or not) when you are making important decisions. You should pick and choose the chapters that are most helpful to you and maybe even save some chapters for a later time when they may be more pertinent.

The book follows students through the decision about whether to go to college in the first place and then through selecting which schools to apply to and where to enroll. But we don't stop there. Once students begin their postsecondary education, they need to choose which courses to take and which field(s) of study to choose as their college major (or majors). They have to make all of these decisions while being bombarded by metrics that provide suggestions ("More selective! Better outcomes!") without really clarifying what students should have in mind when making these important decisions or on what basis they should make one educational choice over other possibilities. We intend to correct the distortions the dominant metrics create and fill in some of these blanks.

We first confront two important questions: Should you go to college? Given that a bachelor's degree has become a major expense for most families, is college worth it? As with all of the questions students have to answer, this one has a standard metric: return on investment. Given how much money you are going to invest by going to college, how much are you going to get back each year as a result of earning a degree? We will show that the numbers that result from calculations of return on investment are often based on preposterous assumptions and misleading data, and we will make some suggestions about how else you can think about the tuition "investment."

The next two chapters address two indicators that are normally used by students who ask which college they should attend. The first is college rankings, which are often assigned by the best-known US ranking organization, *U.S. News & World Report*. Chapter 2 shows that there are better ways to choose which universities to apply to than relying on rankings or even ranking brackets (e.g., the top 50). It also shows why the ranking of a college that interests you should have little influence on how you learn about this college's strengths and weaknesses. We provide a number that applicants should care about much more than they care about ranking as a proxy for expected student outcomes: the graduation rate of an institution. At the same time, we explain why it's helpful for applicants to explore specific features of the colleges and universities that interest them instead of focusing primarily on a single metric, even an improved one like graduation rate.

Chapter 3 addresses a number that many people equate with the quality of the college they're interested in. In deciding which colleges to apply to, you might ask, What is the best college I can get into? The standard indicator of "best" is selectivity, or the percentage of applicants that a particular school admits. Most US colleges admit nearly everyone who applies. But the colleges that people generally assume will give them the biggest advantage in life reject many applicants—sometimes 66%, in the case of the University of California at San Diego, and sometimes 95%, as at Princeton University. The common belief is that this makes Princeton a better college than UC San Diego. We show that even if this is true (for you), it's not because of Princeton's higher selectivity. We replace a bad number with a better number—how much money the college spends on educating each student. This metric is certainly not perfect, but it is far superior to selectivity and the federal government publishes it annually for nearly all colleges and universities. Judging a prospective school by the resources it is willing and able to invest in the typical student's education makes far more sense than doing so by the percentage of applicants that it rejects.

As potential college students think about whether to go to college and then how to pick one, they are also pondering the cost of college. College tuition prices have been rising faster than inflation for two generations and have contributed to disturbingly high levels of overall student debt. The sticker shock that students and families feel after they look at tuition prices makes many of them ask whether they can even afford college. Chapter 4 explains why you should never look at a university's full cost of a year of college as an approximation of what you would actually have to pay to attend. This is true even for middle-class students who assume that their families make too much money for them to receive financial aid. Do not look at tuition sticker prices! This chapter replaces a bad number with a better one: the net cost of attendance, which is the overall amount that a specific student would spend each year on tuition, rent, and food if they enrolled at that college. Net college costs can differ a lot between students from different socioeconomic backgrounds, so the chapter recommends recently developed tools to figure out what attending a given college would actually cost you.

Another logical question at this stage is about the debt many students incur in an effort to finish college and earn a degree. Over 70% of students have some student debt, so debt is more likely than not to affect you. You would naturally ask, Am I the kind of person whose life is going to be changed by student debt? Will I reject my dream career because it might not pay well enough to service my student loans? Or, in order to pay them, will I need to put off starting a family? You may ask these kinds of questions in the context of trying to understand the financial aid material colleges have sent you or a financial aid award letter you received when you were accepted to a college. This chapter is meant to help you understand some of the recent history of student debt, why the growth in that debt has encouraged the proliferation of financial metrics, and how both of these factors are contributing to an environment that may make it seem like your only choice is to pursue a high-wage career.

Up to this point, each chapter has addressed the kinds of questions that people ask prior to attending college. Chapters 6 and 7 assume that you have gotten as far as accepting an admission offer and showing up at a particular school. Then a whole new set of issues arises, as does a whole new set of metrics.

The most important single decision students at American universities make is what field to major in. You usually don't have to pick a
major when you arrive as a first-year student, but you may well have
a general idea about which field most interests you. You may like the
physical sciences or be fairly certain you like visual and graphic arts,
but it can be hard to be sure, partly because high schools offer a much
more limited range of courses than universities do. You will probably
try out a few subject areas, and at most universities you will need to
take courses that satisfy distribution requirements that expose you
to many different fields.

But as you do this, many question may be hanging over your head.
What major will best help me find a well-paying job when I graduate? What major will help me pay off my debt? Am I likely to be able
to complete this major?

Chapter 6 shows that these questions lead many people to another
bad statistic, average wages by college major. This metric can make you
feel that you should pick a major that typically offers higher wages,
even if you're more interested in something else that both you and society value but that pays less. The chapter carefully explains what can
and cannot be inferred from wage-by-major metrics, illustrating the
many ways they can easily lead you astray. Instead of proposing an
alternative statistic, the chapter makes a number of concrete recom-
mendations that would improve the usefulness of popular wage-by-
major indicators and describes how you can make sure that the numbers you're looking at are reliable. It also clarifies that majoring in a
"higher-earning" major often won't increase *your* likelihood of achieving
high earnings, especially if you have a strong preference for majoring
in another field. Choosing a "higher-earning" major may actually lower
your own future wage income compared to the future wages you would
earn if you chose a major you love.

When you arrive at your chosen university, you may quickly learn
that it offers different students very different academic opportunities.

One prominent example is that many universities prevent students who earn low grades in introductory courses from declaring some of their more popular majors. Students that get pushed out of their preferred majors can find themselves in departments that are less well-resourced and, in many cases, offer less intensive learning. Your performance in introductory courses, of course, will be influenced by your high school experience, by your familiarity with the kinds of experiences that suddenly become available to new college students, and by how many hours a week you will have available to study. Students from less-advantaged backgrounds, the very students who might most benefit from stimulating education in a field that interests them, thus tend to face a diminished educational experience at universities that redirect many students into their second- or third-choice major.

None of the popular college rankings provide any information about these restrictions on choice of major or about the kinds of majors that students of different racial and class backgrounds complete. If you belong to an underrepresented racial minority or consider yourself to be a member of the working class, even metrics like "social mobility rankings" are unlikely to be particularly helpful to you. Better metrics would illuminate the degree to which major choices simply echo students' socioeconomic backgrounds at a college and would give a sense of how much money the department that houses your *likely* major will invest in your overall success. While this kind of information isn't widely available, we will help you ask for it from the colleges you're interested in going to. The answer may make a big difference in what you get out of college.

The book ends with a chapter that pulls together a set of indicators that will help you make better judgments about whether, where, and why to go to college and what to study while you're there. We also raise a final question that society does not encourage students and their families to ask but one that is extremely important: Beyond your personal, private monetary gain, what is the value of college?

The reason we pose this question is that much (if not most) of the effect of a college education is what economists call "nonpecuniary," or nonmonetary, and what they call "external," meaning public or social. Nevertheless, both students and their universities face enormous pressure to tailor education to suit financial targets. These targets tend to downplay the social benefits of new or newly distributed knowledge that universities create through their core functions of teaching and research. They also downplay the value of intellectual pleasure, personal development, self-knowledge, and other components of the college experience that are essentially impossible to quantify. When you go to college, you are taking part in a set of elaborate historical practices that have nonmonetary dimensions. Metrics are much better at making monetary benefits visible than at representing nonmonetary and social benefits. The result is that the latter are generally undervalued, both by students and society.

Our conclusion explains that colleges help students live financially prosperous lives while also helping society function better than it otherwise would. Colleges do these two things by generating new personal capabilities, new knowledges across many domains, and new solutions to widespread human crises—in short, by helping students acquire new abilities to solve public problems and to have happy, fulfilling personal lives. The conclusion also describes the material conditions that students and universities need to have in order to get the most out of college. We want to help you ask for and receive adequate housing, adequate food, time away from paid work to study, social and emotional integration into the wider university community, and many other things. Finally, we offer a theory of useful waste that will allow today's students to ask more of their colleges than short-term job training and to identify "wasteful" expenditures that create deeper value for students and for society in the long run.

We have written this book because we believe that better information is and should be available to today's students—and to the wider public. We want you to have more control over your education so that your interests, desires, and preferences will shape your education rather than the other way around. We hope that our discussions will help you see through the fog created by familiar metrics to the realities of today's college life and to the adventure it should offer everyone.

❶

Return on Investment

In 2014, speaking at a General Electric plant in Wisconsin, President Barack Obama offered his thoughts about the value of certain liberal arts degrees. "Folks can make a lot more with skilled manufacturing or the trades than they might with an art history degree." The president immediately qualified his claim: "Now, nothing wrong with an art history degree—I love art history. So, I don't want to get a bunch of emails from everybody. I'm just saying you can make a really good living and have a great career without getting a four-year college education as long as you get the skills and the training that you need."[1]

Art historians, of course, were not pleased. Ann Collins Johns, a professor of art history at the University of Texas at Austin, sent a message to the president noting how her discipline fosters critical reading, writing, and thinking. In response, Obama sent her a handwritten apology: "I was trying to encourage young people who may not be predisposed to a four year college experience to be open to technical training that can lead them to an honorable career."[2] Whatever he intended, his words generated broader questions about the value of a four-year degree that haven't gone away over the years. Should high school students go to college in the first place? Given that college drives so many families into debt, is it worth it?

Among economists who study higher education, the answer to both questions is an unequivocal yes. Earning a college degree, they'll point out, increases lifetime earnings and provides a range of other benefits, including better health and increased levels of civic participation. But with tuition costs and student debt spiraling upward,[3] people want to grab what feels like a concrete number. They've turned to a metric we used to think of mostly in the context of the business world: return on investment (ROI), a metric that compares the gains of an investment to its costs. In the case of the ROI of a college education, it quantifies the typical costs of a bachelor's degree—tuition, housing and dining, transportation, and other expenses—and compares them to the expected salary the student will earn after they earn their degree. ROI calculations say something like this: if you stopped your education at high school you would have earned one million dollars over the next thirty years, but with your bachelor's degree, you will instead earn two million dollars. Subtract the cost of going to college from the net benefit— the extra million dollars—and you get the return on your investment. You can go even further by calculating an annual ROI. Just divide that extra million by the thirty years of your working life, adjusting for the value of future dollars relative to today's dollars. There are many permutations of this basic calculation. All of them purport to help students understand the value of a college degree based on a range of student-specific variables such as their expected tuition cost and their intended major choice.

The ROI metric replaces the deep, individual questions of whether you should go to college and what exactly you want to get out of it with a narrow monetary question: Given how much of my lifetime income I am investing by going to college, what proportion of my investment am I going to get back each year as a result of earning a college degree?

Proponents of these models argue that they create the best metric for helping students make choices about the value of a college degree. Many sound like Zachary First, the managing director of Claremont Graduate University's Drucker Institute. He describes this metric as a kind of "guardrail" for making decisions about college. "If you could just as happily study nursing as nineteenth century German philoso-phy, then by all means, consider what the data tells you about the rela-tive financial security of each option."[4]

Zachary First—and others—are sorely mistaken. They've combined an out-of-place accounting measure with enormous selection bias to create a deeply flawed metric. ROI measures offer a misleading way to measure the value of a college education.[5] Several leading ROI mod-els and data sources rely on bad data that is rife with statistical errors such as nonrepresentative samples and inaccurate self-reports. The most prominent data today—the one that is used in *U.S. News & World Report*, *Forbes*, and *Money*—is the ROI data PayScale and College Score-card publish. Its ubiquity doesn't make up for its poor quality. Let's dig into what makes this data so problematic.

Misleading Data

ROI models are often based upon misleading data. Indeed, one ana-lyst has cautioned that the ROI models produced by PayScale should not be used for "anything beyond cocktail conversation."[6] The PayScale data doesn't have just one source of inaccurate estimates; it has sev-eral layers of misleading data that are being used across several models. In fact, multiple ROI models are drawing upon each other's mislead-ing data to create inaccurate calculations.

Let's start with the work of an important research center, George-town University's Center on Education and the Workforce. Its ROI model draws upon data from the U.S. Department of Education's Col-lege Scorecard to estimate students' future earnings.[7] Significantly, al-though the College Scorecard data is standard and fairly well respected, it is incomplete. For example, the government's reported average "salary after completing" data for each university is calculated only for the 70% of students who receive financial aid from the federal government. This likely skews the picture of schools' actual wage averages.

The Georgetown version of ROI has another problem: it does not consider what wages college students might have earned had they entered the workforce right out of high school instead of enrolling in college. In order to estimate the "return" on a four-year degree, it's important to accurately estimate how much money college graduates would have earned if they hadn't gone to college. Like many other estimates of ROI, the Center on Education and the Workforce approximates the "high school wages" of a given university's students using the average wages of current young people who never went to college. But the kind of people who finish college would likely have had higher-earning careers than the average high school graduate even if they hadn't gone to college. This might seem reasonable at first glance, but once you think about who exactly doesn't go to college in the United States, the meaning of this number starts to dissolve. We've taken what can be an important broad population statistic—the average earnings of people with various levels of education—and pretended that that describes the outcome for a specific person. "MIT students are brilliant," Philip Levine, a professor of economics at Wellesley College, points out. "If they didn't go to college at all, it is unlikely that they would make the minimum wage. What matters is how much is their wage relative to what it would have been had they not gone to college. If you ignore this point, you will get estimates suggesting the MIT has a very high ROI. Maybe that's true, but it's hard to know."[8]

This is a very hard estimate to make, and it is a fundamental methodological problem in the ROI models used to estimate future earnings of undergraduate students. Take PayScale, arguably the best-known compensation service. They define investment in college in what has become the standard ROI way: as the expected future income received after graduating from college. They compare this expected future income to the income of an average student who receives a high school degree. PayScale subtracts the 24-year pay for a 2016 high school graduate from the 20-year pay for a 2016 bachelor's graduate. This calculation, according to PayScale, represents the earnings differential between a high school graduate and college graduate as a 20-year "ROI."[9]

Let's pause to unravel what's really going on in that calculation. Consider an undergraduate at the University of California, Berkeley. On average, students who gain admission to UC Berkeley for an undergraduate degree come from wealthier families and better high schools than students who do not complete a bachelor's degree. Yet PayScale is comparing UC Berkeley students' later-career wages to the average wages of everybody who didn't go to college, a group of people who on the whole have fewer resources and opportunities than UC Berkeley students. Berkeley's students would likely have had much higher-paying careers than average even if they hadn't enrolled at that school because of the same opportunities that helped them get to Berkeley. If we really wanted a better calculation, we should compare the earnings of a UC Berkeley graduate to those of a high school graduate who could have been admitted to UC Berkeley but decided to enter the job market immediately. This is, admittedly, very difficult. There probably aren't too many of those students in the nation. So why does this matter? Failing to account for "positive selection" into certain colleges like UC Berkeley means we've likely overestimated the ROI that the nation's most competitive colleges deliver, further clouding decision-making about college.

Money magazine has sought to address this methodological problem with what it calls a value-added graduation rate.[10] *Money* acknowledges that wealthier students are more likely to graduate regardless of what college they attend. To address this problem, *Money* attempts to take into account a student's economic background and academic preparation: "The higher a school's graduation rate was above the rate that would be predicted for a school with that particular mix of students, the more value that particular college is assumed to have added."[11] *Money* cites a 2013 study by the Organisation for Economic Co-operation and

Development to support its value-added measurement. Yet that study concedes that value-added measurements are limited and are best understood within the context of other qualitative and quantitative indicators, including broader educational contexts, academic performance, retention rates, and quality of education. The fact that one university increases the likelihood that a student will complete their degree does not mean that it will provide better long-run benefits to their students than other universities. After all, degree attainment at an institution might be higher because of lower graduation standards (rather than because of improved learning or greater skill outcomes).[12] In the end, *Money* magazine—like *U.S. News & World Report* and *Forbes*—has relied upon misleading PayScale and College Scorecard data.[13]

That selection bias isn't the only problem with this data. PayScale's ROI model relies on self-reported data. The company generates revenue from what it calls "User Content," which includes the survey data reported by hundreds of thousands of employees from around the United States. Survey respondents are asked to report their jobs, compensation, employer, and educational background. This includes their household income at the time they attended college and their current income. Of course, as numerous studies have demonstrated, self-reported data is particularly vulnerable to errors, especially when it comes to statistics that many people likely haven't thought about in a long time.[14]

PayScale does not explain how it determines the accuracy of these self-reported numbers. Their website provides only two relevant facts. First, self-reported information is solely the responsibility of website users.[15] Second, the company retains the right to modify the data that users provide.[16] So PayScale takes no responsibility for these numbers and even if they did, they're reserving the option to change the data however they want. College applicants should be aware that PayScale's ROI estimates may be based on wage data that could be inaccurate and/or manipulated in opaque ways. (PayScale's main business is providing compensation data to corporate clients using proprietary data sets.)[17]

These data are trotted out to talk about graduates of all sorts of colleges, but is that really who is represented in the data? Hardly. Given PayScale's business model,[18] its data likely overrepresents white collar employees early in their career, a group that is overrepresented in particular industries, geographies, and fields of study. For PayScale's ROI calculations to be accurate and reliable, they would need to be based upon a random selection of individuals both across and within particular universities. Yet this is clearly not how PayScale collects its data: people who participate in PayScale surveys are self-selected. The average number of alumni profiles per university in its database is just 792.[19] Indeed, critics have pointed out that some schools listed among the "top 15" ROI schools have fewer than 100 data points.[20] (For fall 2019, UC Berkeley, a major public university, had a total enrollment of more than 40,000 students). In the absence of large data sets and randomized selection, these ROI calculations will not be representative of the population of college applicants both within and across universities. You cannot rely on their accuracy.

Misleading Estimates

There is another problem. While PayScale's model provides separate calculations for students who earn degrees in different fields at each institution, it fails to provide a reliable measure of the relative value of STEM disciplines (science, technology, engineering, and math) and humanities fields. Two flaws are at the center of the problem. First, PayScale's model omits all college graduates with professional graduate degrees in fields such as medicine, law, public administration, and business and all graduates with PhDs. This isn't a small issue. More than 25% of law degrees are awarded to humanities majors, and humanities majors are generally more likely to earn graduate degrees than most other college graduates.[21] PayScale argues that it is difficult to separate the effect of an undergraduate degree and graduate degree on income: "We can't objectively quantify what portion of their earnings is driven by their undergraduate education and what portion is driven by graduate education."[22] Exactly! This is precisely the point: graduate and professional degrees can dramatically transform the earnings potential of undergraduates across fields, and some undergraduate institutions and degrees are more likely to lead degree recipients to graduate degrees than others. Excluding alumni with graduate degrees thus presents a misleading view and likely skews the ROI estimates of certain colleges and universities (especially liberal arts colleges, which tend to send a greater proportion of their students on to graduate school).

The second problem arises from the time horizon of PayScale's statistics. PayScale calculates return for the twenty years after college graduation, omitting more than half of most college graduates' careers. By limiting its measure of income to two decades, PayScale inflates the relative value of majors such as computer science. While many science and technology majors lead to high earnings early in a career, several studies have demonstrated that humanities majors substantially close the pay gap between younger and older employees over time.[23] The model also does not examine measures of job satisfaction, although a 2014 study of job satisfaction across disciplines found that humanities graduates had some of the highest levels of job satisfaction.[24]

A Misleading Idea of College

We don't want to drag you through all the detailed methodological problems related to calculating the long-term ROI of a college degree. But we do want to convince you not to take such ROI calculations literally, either as a prediction of your own future returns or as a quantification of the abstract worth of a bachelor's degree. ROI models do not do these things with any accuracy or validity. You should not base a major life decision on this metric.

We'll end with perhaps the biggest problem with ROI. Even if it could measure the monetary value of a degree—which it can't—that would be a terrible thing to focus so much attention on. The ROI metric has convinced many people (and policy makers) that college has only private financial value. It doesn't even measure this value accurately, as we've said. But equally seriously, it excludes the nonfinancial benefits of earning a degree. A college degree benefits the families and communities that college students come from or move to after graduating. Graduating from college not only increases student's postgraduate wages, it also improves graduates' long-run health and well-being. Its benefits spill over to nongraduates (a category that includes both people who didn't attend college and those who attended but didn't complete a degree): communities that have higher levels of college degree attainment also have higher wages even for nongraduates and high participation in civic life through activities such as voting.[25] It also offers critical thinking skills and access to higher-order thinking that many people value beyond the contribution of a degree to potential employment earnings. The ROI metric renders these benefits invisible. ROI models encourage students to undervalue nonfinancial benefits and they lead the wider public to misunderstand the value of such benefits.

Should young people go to college? Is a college degree worth it today? These are great questions. Let's debate them. Costs are spiraling. Student debt is rising. Some high school students might be able to have a great career without a four-year degree, as President Obama noted. These ROI metrics, however, don't help people understand this debate nearly as much as they purport to—if they help at all. We suggest that you not use ROI metrics as they are currently circulated. We also suggest that you think about your college choices by taking into account the things college offers other than strict monetary returns. So if using ROI doesn't make much sense, then what does? The next chapters discuss how to make better-informed choices about which college to select, the overall cost of attendance, and how to choose your major.

❷

University Rankings

Each fall, colleges and universities across the United States celebrate a day that isn't a special day on any calendar. On the second Monday of September, a week after Labor Day, *U.S. News & World Report* announces its annual "U.S. News Best Colleges" ranking. The announcement is followed by an explosion of press releases, infographics, and other marketing materials. Higher education public relations teams dream of being able to greet visitors at the local airport with a new giant advertisement about their institution's high ranking. "Number 3 in the Nation for 'Best Value Schools,'" announced Washington D.C.'s Gallaudet University in 2020. "Best in the Midwest" blared the headline from Missouri's Cottey College. The University of California, Berkeley, emailed the good news to all of its enrolled students: "Fourth Best Globally in *U.S. News* Rankings."[1]

Universities pay such close attention to the annual *U.S. News* rankings because of the close attention high school seniors and their families pay to them. A study of the *U.S. News* rankings by economists Michael Luca and Jonathan Smith showed that when a university moves up in the ranking by 1 position (from 22 to 21, say), its average number of applications increases by about 1%, holding everything about the school's educational quality fixed. That may sound small, but in 2017, the average number of annual applications received by top 50 universities was almost 40,000. UCLA received the highest number that year;

more than 100,000 students applied. Every increase in rank a university receives encourages another 400 high school graduates across the country (on average) to apply to that school.[2] Jumping four spots in the *U.S. News* ranking has the potential to increase a university's applications by the same number of first-year students who enroll at Harvard each fall.

The popularity and influence of *U.S. News*'s rankings has spawned dozens of other university rankings published by a wide variety of US media institutions, each of which chooses its own secret sauce of statistics to build their list of top schools. The most important element of the *U.S. News* ranking is a survey of university administrators, such as presidents and deans, that asks them to assess the academic reputation of other schools.[3] The *Princeton Review* ranks the country's best party schools, Niche.com ranks the safest and most "conservative" universities in the United States, and the *Washington Monthly* publishes a list of school rankings titled "Best Bang for the Buck." High school graduates are left to analyze the data from these multiple sources to produce their own list of the country's most outstanding institutions with the goal of finding the right school for them.

But are these rankings useful? Well, they certainly are for college marketing departments. For students and their families choosing where to apply, though, the answer is decidedly mixed. In the next chapter, we'll look at the big issue at the center of many rankings: how selective a college is. First, though, let's tackle a narrower economic question: Is going to a higher-ranked university more likely to lead you to a college degree and a higher-paying job?

It turns out that the answer depends on both a student's family background and their interpretation of what "higher-ranked" means. Here's the bottom line: in most cases, small differences in rankings between colleges and universities are immaterial to future student success. Plus, the much simpler metric of a college's graduation rate will let you separate the proverbial wheat from the chaff.

Small Differences in Rankings

One way that some prospective college students might use rankings is to help them decide between two universities that have similar rank. Consider, for example, a high school senior trying to decide whether to attend Georgetown University or the University of Michigan (we'll call her Jessica to make things easier). *U.S. News* ranked Georgetown 22nd in 2019, five spots higher than Michigan. At the same time, the 2015 Barron's ranking labeled Georgetown "Most Competitive" and ranked Michigan in the next category, called "Highly Competitive."[4] Would Jessica be better off choosing Georgetown, the higher-ranked school?

The answer might depend on the kind of family Jessica comes from. Economists Stacy Dale and Alan Krueger studied this question over two decades by analyzing a detailed survey conducted by the Mellon Foundation in the late 1990s. The survey started with a few cohorts of alumni from about thirty selective US universities, nearly all of which *U.S. News* ranked in the top fifty universities or liberal arts colleges in the country in 2019 (the exceptions were Penn State, which *U.S. News* ranked 59th, and Miami University of Ohio, which it ranked 96th). Tens of thousands of alumni responded to surveys sent to them about twenty years after they left college, reporting (among other things) their annual wages, a key outcome of interest to economists and many prospective college students.

Unsurprisingly, students who attend universities that Barron's ranked higher reported higher earnings than those who attended lower-ranked schools. But there are two possible reasons for that earnings gap. Maybe attending the higher-ranked university provided professional advantages—a better education, connections to high-paying firms and soon-to-be high-earning peers, the reputational advantage of listing the high-ranked university on a résumé—that lead to high mid-career earnings. But higher-ranked universities also have more choice about who to admit into their student body, and many probably choose privileged and/or high-achieving applicants who are already likely to have high-paying jobs in adulthood. Sending all of the students in Cornell's student body to low-ranked universities across the country probably wouldn't ruin their future careers; most of them are already the kind of highly prepared and highly motivated students who will probably find professional success.

If higher-ranked universities provide educational and social experiences that lead their students to high-paying jobs, that might be one reason for Jessica to choose Georgetown over Michigan. But Georgetown students might earn more than Michigan students because they come from wealthier families that connect them to high-paying jobs after graduation or maybe because Georgetown selects students who are more willing to take high-paying finance jobs and work longer hours after graduation. Attending Georgetown might not have anything to do with their eventual career outcomes. In this case, the rankings difference between Georgetown and Michigan might not help Jessica guess which school will lead *her* to a high-paying career.

In their blockbuster study published in 2002, Dale and Krueger used a clever trick to disentangle these two possible explanations. Their goal was to compare the mid-career earnings of people who had a lot in common *before* they attended college to see whether previously similar students ended up with different average earnings after attending differently ranked universities. But how do you identify students who are similar in just the right way so that the only important reason they have different average wages twenty years later is that they attended different universities?

The trick, it turns out, is to compare students who apply to similar sets of universities, as measured by the average SAT score of all the universities each student applies to. The economists called this a "self-revelation model." The students in the Mellon Foundation sample, all of whom ultimately enrolled at high-ranked universities, seem to have had a pretty good idea of their own abilities (and about which universities were likely to admit them), implying that we could get a strong sense of what kinds of lives the students would live just by looking at the schools each of them applied to.

It's a nice trick, but does it work? Here's the key finding from the Dale and Krueger study: students who applied to higher-ranked universities had higher wages, but enrolling at those higher-ranked universities had almost no relationship to their future wages. Dale and Krueger found that there were some applicants, especially those from lower-income families (and, they found in later work, some Black and Latino applicants), who really do benefit from enrolling at higher-ranked universities.[5] Let's not gloss over this: students from these disadvantaged backgrounds do get an economic benefit from enrolling at a slightly higher-ranked university. But on average that's not the case for many of the students at these highly selective universities. Jessica, it seems, probably doesn't have much reason to choose Georgetown over Michigan—at least not because it's going to lead her to higher wages as an alumna.

Large Differences in Rankings

However, there's another very different way that prospective college students could use rankings to help them choose which university to attend. Instead of comparing two schools that have similar rankings, such as Georgetown and Michigan, imagine that Jessica was choosing between universities that have very different rankings, for example Boston University (which *U.S. News* ranked 42nd) and the University of Massachusetts, Boston (UMass Boston, which *U.S. News* ranked 191st). Can Jessica rely on the ranking difference to help her decide between these two schools?

Two education policy experts, Sarah Cohodes and Joshua Goodman, studied that question by analyzing the (unintended) consequences of a Massachusetts scholarship program called the John and Abigail

Adams Scholarship, which offers full tuition scholarships to high school students in the top 25% of their graduating classes if they attend in-state public universities (like the UMass system).[6] Interestingly, though, the universities that Adams scholars are incentivized to attend are not very highly ranked. In Massachusetts alone there are nine private universities that have higher *U.S. News* rankings than the top-ranked public university (UMass Amherst, ranked 70th), from Harvard (ranked 2nd) to the Worcester Polytechnic Institute (ranked 59th) and Clark University (ranked 66th).

Because of the way the Adams Scholarship was structured, students at every Massachusetts high school who were in the 25th percentile of their class got tuition scholarships at public universities, but students in the 26th percentile did not. Since there are no other substantial differences between those two groups of students—after all, the one percentile rank difference probably arose from a tiny difference in the academic performance of students in high school and is essentially almost random—these groups of students constituted a useful test case. What happens when 25th percentile students become eligible for the Adams Scholarship and can receive scholarships to Massachusetts's public universities compared to what happens to the ineligible students whose grades were one percentile lower?

Cohodes and Goodman's first finding is that the Adams Scholarship worked as intended: Adams-eligible students just above the 25th percentile cutoff became much more likely to enroll at Massachusetts public universities than at other schools. But if they hadn't been given the scholarship, most of them would have enrolled at other universities instead, although they might have had to pay higher tuition costs. This led to an unintended consequence of the Adams Scholarship: many of the Adams scholars would have enrolled at *higher*-ranked universities if they had not received the scholarship. Cohodes and Goodman find that about half of the students who switch into UMass universities would have otherwise enrolled at "most," "highly," or "very" competitive universities (as ranked by Barron's). However, no UMass university fell into those categories in the time period Cohodes and Goodman studied.

Surprisingly, Cohodes and Goodman found that even though the eligible students who enrolled at public universities received the $1,400 annual Adams Scholarship, it proved very costly in the long run. While fewer than 40% of the 26th percentile students who attended other universities dropped out without earning a college degree, the students in the 25th percentile who were induced to enroll at the UMass system became about 30 percentage points *more* likely to drop out of college and fail to earn a degree. In other words, the Adams Scholarship led a group of Massachusetts students to enroll at lower-ranked public universities with relatively lower graduation rates than the schools they were otherwise going to go to and as a result, they ended up becoming less likely to graduate college themselves. They accepted the Adams Scholarship only to drop out of UMass.

The consequences of the Adams Scholarship suggest an important reason for Jessica to treat the rankings difference between Boston University and UMass Boston seriously. Attending UMass could increase her likelihood of dropping out before earning her bachelor's degree, which is a big risk for her economic future. We'll talk more about why students at some lower-ranked universities are less likely to complete college degrees in the next chapter, but this example rules out college costs as a potential explanation; after all, the UMass students were more likely to drop out despite their full scholarships.

Zachary Bleemer, one of our coauthors, studied a similar program in California, the Eligibility in the Local Context (ELC) Program.[7] Under that program, students in the top 4% of their high school classes were virtually guaranteed admission to whichever of seven California public universities they applied to. Eligible students weren't given scholarships, but the universities that ELC incentivized students to attend— the University of California campuses at Santa Barbara, Irvine, Davis, and San Diego—were all highly ranked relative to the alternative schools for the eligible students; all of those schools had national *U.S. News* rankings in the range of 30 to 41 in 2019.

At California's top high schools (ranking schools by their students' SAT scores), the ELC program rarely changed students' admissions outcomes at any of the participating universities. Regardless of whether those students were in the top 1 or 5 or 10% of their classes, nearly all of them were already able to get in to highly ranked University of California campuses, whether or not the program guaranteed their admission. The students who benefited from ELC the most came from the bottom SAT quartile of California high schools, since many of the top students from those schools would have otherwise been rejected from many University of California campuses and enrolled at low-ranked local teaching-oriented universities or community colleges. The ELC program enabled them to go to high-ranked research universities instead.

Using a research design similar to the one used in Massachusetts study—that is, comparing 4th percentile ELC-eligible students to 5th percentile ineligible students—Bleemer showed that the program pulled hundreds of eligible students each year from ever enrolling at much lower-ranked colleges and universities—schools with higher admissions rates, lower average SAT scores, and lower graduation rates—and led them to enroll at highly ranked University of California campuses instead. The enrollment effect of this California policy, then, is opposite of the Adams Scholarship: the ELC program led targeted applicants to enroll at higher-ranked universities than they would have if they hadn't been eligible for admission through ELC.

As you might expect, then, the ELC program's impact on student outcomes was exactly the opposite of the impact of the Adams Scholarship. Among the students who enrolled at less-selective colleges and universities because they weren't eligible for ELC, only about half of them had earned a college degree within five years of graduating from high school. In contrast, among the otherwise similar students who enrolled at higher-ranked University of California campuses because of the ELC program, about three-quarters had earned a BA within five years. Students who enrolled at the University of California also ended up with much higher wages early in their careers and they were more likely to enroll in graduate school in their mid-20s. That combination will likely lead to large long-run economic benefits.

The ELC program mattered for different students in different ways. It all depends on which schools the ELC participants would have enrolled at if not for the ELC program. Some students would have enrolled at universities that had similar graduation rates and rankings as the UC campuses they attended because of their ELC eligibility, but the ELC program didn't seem to change their educational or employment outcomes at all. That is because similarly ranked universities provide similar benefits. The students who would have otherwise enrolled at somewhat lower-ranked universities earned small benefits in terms of degree completion and wages. But students who would have otherwise enrolled at unranked universities—such as community colleges or most of the state's teaching-oriented California State University schools (which *U.S. News* ranks separately as "Regional Universities")—gained substantially by attending high-ranked universities under the ELC program.

Bleemer found that the benefits of attending "better" schools consistently scale with a simple measure of university quality: the graduation rate. Imagine a student who is choosing between two universities, one of which has a higher five-year graduation rate by 5% compared to the other. If the student chooses to enroll at the school with the higher graduation rate, then they themselves are more likely to earn a college degree within five years by about 5%. If a student goes to a school with a 20% higher graduation rate, then on average she becomes 20% more likely to finish her degree. Going to schools with higher graduation rates also leads students to proportional increases in wages in the early years of their career, likely both because their students are more likely to earn degrees and because schools with higher graduation rates tend to provide more valuable education to their students. Several other studies have also shown that graduation rates provide a surprisingly useful proxy for comparing the educational and economic impacts of very different universities.[8]

The studies of both the Adams Scholarship and the ELC program provide an important counterweight to the findings from the Mellon Foundation study we discussed a few pages ago. When there is a big difference in rankings—like that between UMass Boston and Boston University or between San Diego State University (ranked 127th) and UC San Diego (ranked 41st)—the rankings gap is suggestive of another important difference: schools with very different rankings are almost certain to also have very different graduation rates. And attending a university with a much higher graduation rate seems to discourage students from dropping out and lead them to higher early-career wages—and likely also to later-career advantages.

Gaming the Rankings

Graduation rates are at least as helpful as rankings in identifying important differences in student outcomes at different universities. There is another reason to rely on graduation rates rather than university rankings as a basis for making important choices about where to go to college: universities can "game" rankings in ways that may not be helpful to potential students.

Baylor University has become a classic example of how universities game their rankings. About 10% of the *U.S. News* ranking is determined by the average standardized test scores of each university's incoming class. In 2008, Baylor identified an innovative way to raise the average SAT scores of its freshman class. In October that year, *The Baylor Lariat* reported how the school did it:

An e-mail sent in June to incoming freshmen stated that students who chose to retest [for the SAT] would automatically receive a $300 credit to the bookstore. If a student scored 50 [more] points or higher [than their SAT score as an applicant] on the retest, they received an additional $1,000 a year to their scholarship package. . . . Of the 861 students who retested this summer, 151 students improved their score by at least 50 points and received the $1,000 scholarships.[9]

In other words, Baylor paid its incoming students to retake the SAT *after they had already been admitted* in order to publicly report a higher average test score. And they succeeded: the school's average SAT score increased by 10 points as a result of their retaking policy. A Baylor administrator told the *New York Times*, "Every university wants to have great SAT scores. Every university wants to be perceived as having a high-quality class. . . . Are we happy our SAT scores went up? Yes."[10] That may be, but it's unclear why any student's opinion of Baylor should be inflated by Baylor's SAT retaking policy.

There are many ways to game university rankings, some more expensive than others, although they all consume university resources. Some universities try harder than others. In 2014, *Boston* magazine reported that Northeastern University had put a premium on "glad-handing" high-ranked university presidents to try to convince them of Northeastern's elite educational quality and improve their *U.S. News* peer assessment scores in the mid-2000s.[11] In 2009, *Inside Higher Ed* reported that Clemson University uses a variety of financial tricks to change the apparent generosity of its financial aid and faculty compensation policies and increases the sizes of certain classes in a way that avoids the specific definitions of class size that *U.S. News* uses.[12] The next chapter presents examples of how universities game their selectivity statistics, another common component of university rankings.

Because graduation rates are harder to game than many of the other rankings metrics, they provide a more reliable measure of the educational services colleges provide to their students. Moreover, when universities work to improve their graduation rate, that investment generally improves students' actual experiences at the university and an increased proportion of each class earns a degree as a result. To be clear, there are ways to artificially inflate graduation rates that don't benefit students. For example, a university could lower its academic standards (which we'll discuss more in chapter 7) or admit fewer lower-income students (who might be less likely to graduate from college no matter which institution they attend).[13] Still, on balance, the fact that some components of ranking systems can be gamed is another reason to turn elsewhere to learn which universities most benefit their students.

Conclusion: Do We Really Need Rankings at All?

This chapter has partly focused on the economic outcomes of where you go to college—on what happens to a student's likely future earnings when they attend a higher-ranked university. As the previous chapter made clear, economics isn't everything. There are a lot of reasons to go to college other than higher future earnings. But for students looking to use rankings to help them choose between universities on economic grounds, this chapter has shown that rankings can be easily replaced by a more straightforward measure of quality: graduation rates. Graduation rates are readily available for all four-year colleges and universities, not just those ranked by media organizations, and the research discussed above suggests that they do a better job of helping applicants distinguish which universities will lead to a bachelor's degree and high-paying employment.

As with rankings, small differences in schools' graduation rates—like the average difference of 6 percentage points in the graduation rates of the 30th and 60th "best" universities in *U.S. News*'s 2019

ranking—don't tell you much about long-run economic outcomes, although lower-income or underrepresented minority students may
benefit from enrolling at institutions with slightly higher graduation
rates. When the difference in graduation rates is large, though, or when
the alternative is an institution like a community college, most of which
do not publish comparable graduation rates (but where most students
earn only a two-year degree), the difference matters. Attending a university with a much higher graduation rate confers important economic
advantages in the form of higher postgraduate wages. As a metric, graduation rates can be a helpful tool for future-oriented college applicants
and can usefully replace the statistically less reliable university rankings
that media organizations publish.

❸

Selectivity

Do you want to go to college or do you want to go to a "good" college? Is your main goal to get a solid bachelor's degree or is your goal to get one from a place that everyone agrees is a cut above?

At first, the answer seems obvious: you need to go to a good college. For decades, research has consistently shown that you should go to college and finish it and also that you get more economic benefit from finishing a good college than you do from finishing a weaker one.[1] Measuring intellectual and other benefits is a lot harder, but as we show in our other chapters, researchers generally find that you learn more in a good college than in a mediocre one.

Here's the harder but more important question: What exactly is a good college? This turns out to be a deep and complicated issue. The answer depends on who the applicant is and what they are trying to do. Because of the difficulty of this question, most people gravitate to one simple number to capture the quality of a college, often its rank.

College rankings try to reduce a college's quality to its specific rung in a hierarchy of schools. Rankings are made up of many different numbers that measure many different things: total number of scientific prizes, class size, faculty salaries, maybe the number of books in the library. Few people think that any one of these numbers is, by itself, a good stand-in for the overall quality of a college—with one giant exception: selectivity.

Selectivity measures the share of applicants to a college that the college rejects. It's usually expressed the other way around, as an admission rate. For fall 2019, the University of California, Berkeley accepted 16.4% of its applicants, while the University of California San Diego accepted 32.3%.[2] There's a fair amount of informal evidence that most people equate selectivity with quality. The better college is, to many of us, the more selective college. We can boil down why we think UC Berkeley is better than UC San Diego to this one simple number: it rejects a greater share of its applicants. This selectivity number is so widely used that Google displays it as one of the three initial features of any university you search for.

In the United States, selectivity and status are joined at the hip. The issue for many applicants is less the question "Does UC Berkeley have better teaching and research than UC San Diego and more motivated students, which means that I'll end up smarter by learning more?" and more a belief that "Everyone knows Berkeley is really hard to get into, so I will have more status myself, be seen as smarter, and get a better job if I go to Berkeley." Paul Tough defines the traditional admissions rule as "go to the most selective schools that will admit you, period."[3]

A Problem in California

The University of California is an interesting example for us. More than most state university systems, it has a set of similar campuses with the same overall mission and student population. UC's vision has been that it is "One University" of similar research campuses rather a flagship or two surrounded by regional colleges, as is the case with the large state systems in New York, North Carolina, and Texas, for example. Seven of UC's nine undergraduate campuses are members of the American Association of Universities, which is a select club of the roughly sixty top research universities. We know that the University of California isn't a typical public college system, but it has the advantage of offering a formal company of equals that one might expect would have led to a public perception that all UC campuses offer equal educational quality.

Contrary to the "One University" idea, the public generally believes that UC campuses vary greatly in prestige, stature, and quality of students. When some UC students made a video called "UC Stereotypes Explained" (2014), they reproduced the same campus hierarchy that was already in place in the 1980s: the flagships at Berkeley and Los Angeles on the top and Merced joining Riverside and Santa Cruz at the bottom.[4]

Those of us who work in the University of California system know that the high-quality programs we care about are distributed throughout the system. The biosciences are as strong at San Diego as they are at Berkeley, to take just one example. So why is the UC campus hierarchy so fixed in people's minds and why has it remained so stable over years or decades? The dominant factor is the stability of levels of selectivity. The most noticeable difference among UC campuses is how much harder it is to get into UCLA and UC Berkeley than it is to get admitted to Riverside and Santa Cruz.

This is also a self-fulfilling prophecy. The same lore about the flagships has circulated for a few generations now—that Berkeley and UCLA are much more selective than the others in large part because they are seen as the best (and have the highest overall rankings). But they have the highest overall rankings and are seen as the best because they are the hardest to get into. San Diego, which rivals and sometimes surpasses Berkeley and UCLA in rankings of academic quality, has never quite achieved the position of a "third flagship," most likely because its selectivity rate is similar to those of Santa Barbara, Davis, and Irvine. This group of campuses are distinctly more selective than the UC schools we just mentioned: Riverside, Santa Cruz, and Merced, the newest UC campus.

In our experience, if you ask a Californian which are the best UC schools, the list will almost exactly track this selectivity ranking. UC's

FIGURE 3.1.

Niche's 2018 college rankings
for the University of California system

RANK	SCHOOL NAME	NICHE OVERALL GRADE	ACCEPTANCE RATE	SAT RANGE	ACADEMICS GRADE	NET PRICE	TOTAL STUDENTS
1	UCLA	A+	17.3%	1180–1470	A+	$13,816	29,004
2	UC Berkeley	A+	16.9%	1250–1510	A+	$16,601	26,622
3	UC Santa Barbara	A+	32.6%	1090–1360	A	$16,211	20,243
4	UC Davis	A	38%	1070–1340	A	$16,841	27,453
5	UC San Diego	A	38%	1070–1340	A+	$14,933	25,922
6	UC Irvine	A	38.7%	1030–1290	A	$14,662	24,854
7	UC Riverside	A–	55.6%	980–1210	A–	$13,365	18,279
8	UC Santa Cruz	A–	50.3%	1050–1300	A–	$17,550	15,823
9	UC Merced	B+	60.7%	900–1120	B+	$13,350	6,164

Source: "University of California System," Niche, n.d., accessed May 13, 2018, https://www.niche.com/colleges/university-of-california-system/.

Office of the President participates in rankings that sharply stratify the campuses, and services such as Niche rank UC campuses in a nearly exact replication of their selectivity rankings.[5]

In 2018, Niche gave UC Santa Barbara a lower "academics grade" than UC San Diego but an overall ranking that is higher than UC San Diego's (fig. 3.1). It appears that Santa Barbara's higher selectivity that year (only 32.6% of applicants accepted, compared to San Diego's 38%) boosted its rank. In Niche's 2020 tables, San Diego had fallen to number 6.[6]

One could argue that perceived status tracks selectivity for other university groups such as the members of the Ivy League or the Big 10. Yale's 4.6% admission rate to the class of 2025 is lower than Cornell's 10.3%; Michigan at 26% is more selective than Indiana at 72%. Here too, perceived prestige tracks selectivity.

The stakes of selectivity numbers increase when parents, students, and scholars link them not only to prestige but also to future wages. An important recent study of the labor market effects of attending selective colleges by two economists starts like this:

> Students who attend higher-quality colleges earn more on average than those who attend colleges of lesser quality. However, it is unclear why this differential occurs. Do students who attend more selective schools learn skills that make them more productive workers, as would be suggested by human capital theory? Or, consistent with signaling models, do higher-ability students—who are likely to become more productive workers—attend more selective colleges?[7]

Whether the "higher-quality" college increases wages by supporting better learning or by admitting students who already learned more in high school, the authors of this influential article assumed that "more selective" is functionally the same as "higher quality." (Confusingly, the economics literature tends to equate selectivity with higher average cognitive ability even while arguing that selectivity is more signal than substance.[8])

Here's another example from the University of California. For figure 3.2, we used the U.S. Department of Education's College Scorecard to identify median wages at eight UC campuses. Median salaries for our sample align fairly closely with the public perception of the status and the selectivity rankings of the campuses. The students who went to Berkeley earned nearly 10% more than their San Diego counterparts ten years after graduation. Don't these data make a clear case for the use of selectivity as an indicator of quality? Actually, no. But we have to go through some discussion to see why not.

FIGURE 3.2.

Median wages of University of California students by campus ten years after matriculation (among those receiving federal financial aid)

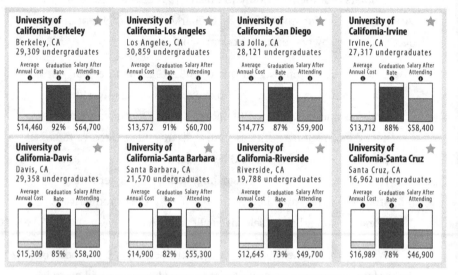

Source: U.S. Department of Education College Scorecard, accessed August 23, 2019, https:// collegescorecard.ed.gov/.

Those who say selectivity is a valid indicator of quality can offer a simple reason why: more selective schools reject more weak students, so the remaining pool is of better academic quality. That would be true whether we think "weaker" students are those who have lower cognitive ability or those who have worse preparation.

Notice that the emphasis on selectivity suggests that college is more about selecting existing talent than about developing new or further talent. Later in this chapter, we'll suggest a measure to replace selectivity that focuses on a college's financial ability to develop talent.

Remember that selectivity is measured as the share of applicants a school selects from the overall pool. In 2018, when UC Berkeley accepted only 16.9% of applicants, it took only about half the share of applicants that UC San Diego accepted (fig. 3.1). We might assume that Berkeley rejected the weaker half of their top third of applicants, all of whom, in theory, could get into San Diego. In this narrative, Berkeley is better than San Diego because all of Berkeley's students were similar to those in the top half of San Diego admits, while San Diego also admitted many students who couldn't get into Berkeley. This would presumably drag the average San Diego student down below the academic attainment of the average Berkeley student. In this conventional view, the typical UC San Diego student would be weaker than the typical UC Berkeley student. So Berkeley's higher selectivity makes Berkeley's student body better than UC San Diego's.

Another assumption reinforces this belief. *U.S. News* (to give one example) is typical in its assertion that "a school's academic atmosphere is determined in part by students' abilities and ambitions."[9] Thus, we seem to have support for our view that UC Berkeley has a more ambitious and capable student body because its admissions office rejected the weaker students among their applicants. The assumption that many people make based on Berkeley's selection rate is that a typical group of students at Berkeley will be more ambitious and capable. In short, these people assume, Berkeley will have a higher percentage of students who will be more academically prepared, find better jobs, help their peers with better connections, and the like. Therefore, this view concludes, Berkeley is a better university than San Diego.

The Trouble with Selectivity

In reality, this commonsense belief is wrong. We are about to explain why. Our goal is to convince you *not* to focus on a school's selectivity rate when you are choosing a college. If you must use a number, we'll offer you a better one than selectivity—funds spent on instruction for the typical student (see below). We'll also try to help you to think about college without looking at numbers at all. Choosing a university should be a highly personalized process that reflects a person's individual strengths, needs, and goals. It should be based on detailed self-reflection and rich descriptions of each college or university as its own specific kind of place.

First, let's look at the technical problems with the selectivity metric. Selectivity numbers do not measure the thing they say they measure. They *say* they measure the quality of admitted students (and, making another leap in logic, the quality of the college that admits them). They are actually measuring something quite different: the percentage of a given college's applicant pool that gains admission. As we'll see, a college can automatically achieve a very tough selectivity rate by increasing its applicant pool with prospective students whom it will then reject.

Selectivity is a supply-and-demand ratio. It is calculated as the supply of seats available at the college divided by the demand for those seats (the number of applicants). The selectivity metric represents only the relative demand for a university's supply. It says nothing about the "quality" of the students who are admitted compared to those who are rejected.

For example, in the mid-2010s, the University of Chicago began to receive 30,000 applications each year. The 2,356 students they admitted are statistically very similar to the next 2,356 students they rejected.[10] The selectivity figure is an arithmetic ratio that does not say anything substantive about the differences between the students who are admitted and those who are rejected, particularly around the rejection threshold.

Second, as we've said already, the relationship between selectivity and quality is circular. A college's perceived high quality attracts more applicants, which creates more rejections, which increases selectivity, which increases perceived quality, which attracts more applicants. This circularity means that universities have an interest in manipulating their selectivity figures—and they do manipulate them.

In 2010, a reporter at the *Chronicle of Higher Education*, Eric Hoover, dug into a particular case of such manipulation at the University of Chicago. He began by noting that "measuring quality is difficult; measuring quantity is as easy as counting. The more apps a college receives, and rejects, the more impressive it seems." Hoover reported that the University of Chicago was tired of watching its competitors climb the selectivity ladder. It had always stressed how unique and special it was—how nerdy, how intellectually intense. Chicago was the opposite of a generic elite school: it had a strong personality and a strong academic focus and was rewarded with a similarly focused applicant pool. This meant that as recently as 2005, it had "only" 9,100 applicants, about a third as many as rivals such as Stanford and Brown.[11]

The university's strong, specific identity was reflected in its admissions strategy:

> For years, Chicago's admissions office emphasized the university's distinctiveness, sending offbeat mailings, like a postcard ringed with a coffee stain. Its application has long included imaginative essay prompts, like "If you could balance on a tightrope, over what landscape would you walk? (No net)." This became known as the "Uncommon Application," in contrast to the Common Application, the standardized form that allows students to apply to any of hundreds of participating colleges.[12]

In 2009, a relatively new president, Robert Zimmer, decided that Chicago needed a bigger and more typically impressive applicant pool. He hired a new admissions director, James Nondorf.

> Mr. Nondorf's first priority was to create a recruitment booklet that contained many photographs of students engaged in group activities, including music, dance, tennis, and football. Later Chicago sent tailored letters to students who had expressed an interest in the arts or in medicine. Admissions officers talked up pre-professional opportunities and career

preparation. Visiting families received special rates from the Hilton, where a letter from Mr. Nondorf and a pouch of chocolates awaited them. Over the last year, Chicago's admissions representatives visited about twice as many high schools as they had the previous year. . . . Chicago officials have cited many reasons for [2009–2010's] application explosion, including the popularity of President Obama, who taught at the university. But some credit should go to Royall & Company, a direct-marketing firm the university hired . . . to help conduct an expansive recruitment campaign.[13]

The University of Chicago's selectivity skyrocketed. Within five years, it had pushed down its acceptance rate to 8% of applicants, far below the 40% figure of 2005. Not coincidentally, Chicago has risen steadily in *U.S. News* rankings, to number 6 by 2018.[14]

The key to the increase in selectivity was the increased size of the applicant pool. In the first year of the new marketing campaign, the size of that pool increased by 43%, to 31,000. This is not the same thing as an increase in the quality of the admitted students. All we know is that the University of Chicago changed its marketing techniques to attract mainstream applicants and tripled the size of its applicant pool from what it was in 2005. It then accepted about the same total number of applicants that it always had. (It did increase its undergraduate numbers somewhat in later years). The university became more selective because it rejected a higher share of an artificially expanded applicant pool.

Here is a third problem with selectivity: it's the cheapest rankings boost around. Universities need to spend real money if they want to rise in the rankings by shrinking class sizes and hiring more tenure-track faculty or by building state-of-the-art laboratories for top researchers. For example, the University of Southern California, which has been raising and spending money on big-ticket science for twenty years, has gone from 41st to 21st in the *U.S. News* rankings in that time.[15] But each of its major coups in attracting major research teams can cost hundreds of millions of dollars for facilities and run tens of millions a year in new overhead costs.[16] In contrast, increasing applicant pools via outreach and branding costs very little. More important, it doesn't benefit enrolled students at the university. Universities can certainly do both, of course, but it's much less expensive to move up in the rankings by growing the number of students you reject than by building a better school for the students you take.

Selectivity as Distraction

So far, we have identified three problems with selectivity as an indicator of quality: it only measures demand in relation to supply, it is easily gamed, and it can be a cheap substitute for investments in teaching and research. Perhaps for these reasons, *U.S. News & World Report* stopped using selectivity as an explicit component of their university rankings in 2019, although they continued to display admissions rate statistics for each college and university.

We also need to consider a fourth problem. Selectivity can encourage standardization. The University of Chicago is again an example of a college that got more applications by downplaying its distinctive identity and becoming more typical, recognizable, and attractive to a large group of applicants. But that distinctive identity is one of the main reasons to go to Chicago. Admissions consultant Jeff Levy explains:

> [The University of Chicago] is the first college in fifteen years to successfully infiltrate the top ten colleges that never change position.
>
> Why is this terrible? Because students who belong at UChicago can no longer get in. The college isn't any better than it used to be, and some would say this new homogenized version is less distinguishable than it once was from its peer

institutions. For the idealists among us—those who believe that colleges should celebrate what makes them unique and that applicants should apply to those colleges where they are a great fit—UChicago is one for the loss column.[17]

Levy is right that standardization can discourage the quirky originality on which creativity, productivity, intellectual pleasure, and valuable job skills generally depend.

One final issue is probably the most serious of all. Selectivity diverts public attention from a fundamental source of educational quality. It does this by tying the basic indicator of college success—completing a bachelor's degree—to the ability of a college to reject a high percentage of applicants, thus distracting us from a college's financial capacity to spend enough money on each student's instruction to develop their individual talents.

It's well known that graduation rates are higher at more selective colleges and universities. The National Center for Educational Statistics generated a helpful chart of the relationship (fig. 3.3).[18] Not only do graduation rates vary by race, gender, and socioeconomic status—poorer students, racial minorities, and males are all at greater risk of dropping out of college before earning a degree—they also vary dramatically by the institution's selectivity. At public community colleges, for example, which are generally open admission (every qualified student is accepted), only 25% of students earn a two-year degree within four years.[19]

One particularly detailed analysis, which William G. Bowen, Matthew M. Chingos, and Michael S. McPherson published in 2009 as *Crossing the Finish Line*, shows that 84% of students graduate in six years from the universities the authors identified as more selective. Only 56% do the same for their less selective group. That is a big difference. Selectivity *is* a better predictor of graduation rates than other factors like the quality of the student's high school.

FIGURE 3.3.

Graduation rate within six years for first-time, full-time US students seeking bachelor's degrees at four-year postsecondary institutions by admission rate of institution for the cohort who began college in 2010

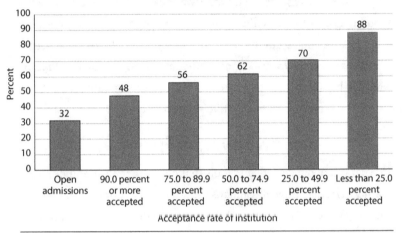

Source: National Center for Education Statistics, "Undergraduate Retention and Graduation Rates," last updated May 2022, https://nces.ed.gov/programs/coe/indicator/ctr

But the catch is that while there is a measurable *correlation* between selectivity and graduation rates—higher selectivity tracks with higher graduation rates—there is no *causal* relation. Bowen, Chingos, and McPherson found that selectivity is not the feature that improves college success rates. They determined this by running a simulation in which they retroactively "rejected" all students below a chosen threshold of grades the students received in high school. They then compared graduation rates for their "more qualified" remaining group that was just on the higher side of the threshold. What the researchers found was startling. Most people assume that more selective colleges have better graduation rates for the simple reason we've discussed—they screen out the weaker students from the very beginning. That's not what this simulation found. In this study, retroactively "rejecting" weaker students did not change the simulated graduation rates at the most selective universities. It produced "only a tiny gain in the overall graduation rate" for the next group of schools, and it increased the graduation rate by just six points at the least selective schools.[20]

In fact, the surprising "reality is that graduation rates vary dramatically across universities even when we look [only] at students with good high school grades and impressive test scores."[21] This is because it is not true that students are more likely to graduate at selective schools because they were stronger students to begin with. Graduation rates are higher at selective colleges because of something about the colleges that affects students while they are there.

Selectivity versus Spending

So what is it about selective schools that helps students graduate? This is a mystery that Bowen, Chingos, and McPherson unfortunately did not try to solve.[22] And yet they did show correlations between improved graduation rates and features like access to scholarly communities in honors colleges such as Penn State's Schreyer Honors College and City University of New York's Macaulay Honors College.[23] Other studies show that well-staffed living arrangements, individual advising, tutoring staff, psychological and peer counseling services, better-paid teaching assistants, and more departmental advising do help students learn.[24] These student and academic services all cost money.

Another major expense for colleges and universities is financial aid. The net price of a college education is the actual price students pay after aid is deducted from the official cost of tuition (the sticker price) (we'll come back to this topic in the next chapter). Bowen, Chingos, and McPherson found that the less students actually pay, the more likely they are to graduate.[25]

Although levels of financial aid vary from college to college, average financial aid is generally proportional to the college's overall financial resources.[26] Wealthier colleges can directly improve graduation rates by spending more money on financial aid than their less-affluent counterparts can. A student with more grants, fewer loans, and less financial "self-help expectation" (an amount the student must find a way to pay themselves) can work less while in college and therefore study more. A student who studies more and who has more flexibility in their schedule to pour extra effort into courses that are hard for them is more likely to do well academically and to graduate. It can be cheaper for certain students (especially if their family household income is less than $100,000) to go to an expensive private university like Stanford, which has a large endowment and generous financial aid, than to the University of Michigan, which charges about one-third the tuition but offers less financial aid. It's not surprising that Stanford also has a higher graduation rate than the (also excellent) University of Michigan.

This exemplifies our main point: the quality of a student's education has very little to do with what percentage of applicants their college rejected and a lot more to do with how much money that college spends on each of its students.[27] College officials generally don't like to talk about the relationships between money and learning. One famous book discussed the problem of "limited learning" by talking about everything *except* unequal funding.[28] And yet a few studies have gathered evidence that supports our point. First, we have broad evidence that selectivity is often highly correlated with how much colleges spend on students.[29] Second, one of the most thorough studies of racial disparities found a positive relationship between the share of white students, graduation rates, and funding levels. It found that "white students are increasingly concentrated today, relative to population share, in the nation's 468 most well-funded, selective four-year colleges and universities while African American and Latino students are more and more concentrated in the 3,250 least well-funded, open-access, two- and four-year colleges."[30] When the authors linked this sorting into different strata of colleges to their funding, they created figure 3.4. The vast majority of African American and Latino students

FIGURE 3.4.

Instructional spending per student by selectivity category

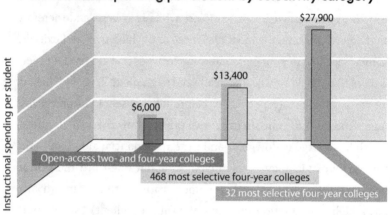

Source: Anthony P. Carnevale, Ban Cheah, and Andrew R. Hanson, *The Economic Value of College Majors* (Washington, DC: Georgetown University Center on Education and the Workforce, 2015).

entering college in the 2000s went to nonselective institutions that spent less than 25% of what the 82 most selective colleges spent on instruction on average.

But did these expenditure gaps affect outcomes for these students? These authors answer with a resounding yes (fig. 3.5). Even accounting for variation in students' academic preparedness before enrolling at different universities, they found that attending a more selective school significantly increased the chance that a student would graduate. The authors also provided evidence that higher graduation rates translate into earnings advantages for all graduates of a particular college, an idea we'll return to in the next chapter.

We wanted to further explore whether money spent per student does a better job of predicting graduation rates than selectivity does, so we turned to statistics.[31] Here's what we found: two pieces of information about each university that a prospective student could possibly attend—the schools' instructional expenditures per student and its ad-

FIGURE 3.5.

Graduation rates for similarly qualified students by selectivity category

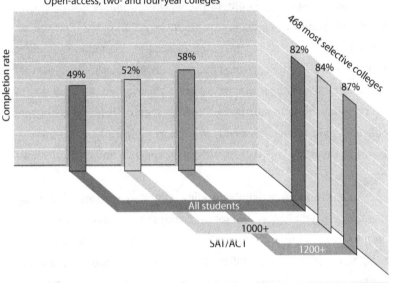

Open-access, two- and four-year colleges

468 most selective colleges

Completion rate

49% 52% 58% 82% 84% 87%

All students

1000+

SAT/ACT

1200+

Source: Anthony P. Carnevale, Ban Cheah, and Andrew R. Hanson, *The Economic Value of College Majors* (Washington, DC: Georgetown University Center on Education and the Workforce, 2015).

missions rate—appear to be similarly informative about the quality of those universities as measured by graduation rate. After all, as we discussed above, universities that look good on one of those measures usually look good on the other. But level of spending on instruction appears to be a much more useful piece of information about universities if the student also has other information about the universities, such as average SAT scores and where the school is located. If you know these other things, selectivity doesn't add any new valuable information, while knowing how much a university or college spends on instruction does.

In other words, selectivity doesn't actually measure anything fundamental about university quality, so knowledgeable students can't learn very much from it. The amount a college spends on each student also doesn't tell you everything, but it tells you something much more relevant to the quality of education than selectivity alone does. For example, although Stanford and UC Berkeley enroll comparable students and UC Berkeley is one of the wealthiest public institutions in the world, Stanford spends four times more per student.[32] To take another example: if you are planning to start at a community college before transferring to a private nonprofit college, you should know that the community college spends 30 cents on average per student for every dollar the four-year private college spends.[33] How much a specific college or university spends to support their students' instruction is one of the most important numbers prospective university students need to have.

Another important detail: spending on student services—things like mentoring, psychological counseling, health services, and tutoring—also seems to contain useful information that is predictive of students' success, especially at private universities. This makes sense if we think of student services as instructional support that also helps their learning.[34] To oversimplify only a bit, instructional and student services spending are two sides of the same education coin. In both cases, serious investments help students learn, advance, and graduate.

You Select the College

Of course, college is complicated and various factors work together to make it good or not so good for any particular student. Whether a student succeeds in college (and later at work) is affected by the quality of their high school, the racial discrimination they've endured, the amount of free time they have, their social world, their parents' level of education, their family's income, and so on. But we can conclude some important things. People are wrong to think that the more selective college is clearly the better college. "More selective" simply means it rejected a higher share of its applicants. It makes more sense to say that highly selective Cornell is "better" than less-selective Brooklyn College because it spends much more money on the education of each of its students. More selective colleges benefit their students by providing high-quality instruction, student-related research, individual contact with full-time professors, and comprehensive student support, all of which cost serious money. These in turn make the college better for its students, and lead to better outcomes.

When you choose the colleges you want to apply to, you should think about what you really love to do and what you really want to study. You should read detailed descriptions about the colleges you are interested in and talk to people with firsthand knowledge about educational life at those places. You should look at data about how much each college spends per student on education. The U.S. Department of Education collects these data in its College Scorecard, but they're not easy to find (you have to download these data yourself). You can always ask college representatives about this metric for their school.[35] Instructional expenditure will influence who would be teaching you: will it be tenured professors or graduate students or adjunct instructors? Expenditures will affect how much time your instructors have to prepare each course (tenured professors teach fewer courses per term and have more time to prepare). It will affect how much time your instructor has to spend on each class and thus how much time they can spend on you. Dollars per student is reflected in the level of technology available, how much free advising and tutoring you can get, and how many courses are offered in your specific area of interest. Dollars per student show up in how much staff support an instructor gets for course registration, routine advising, and assistance with digital course materials. That same money helps determine whether you can participate in research as an undergraduate. Spending averages across the campus tell you quite a bit, and departmental expenditures, which can vary, may tell you even more.[36]

In short, you should care a lot about instructional resources in your area of interest. If you can't get this information, ask why not and encourage the colleges you apply to and especially the one you attend to offer this information publicly.

While money isn't everything, the focus on selectivity has distracted the country from the crucial funding questions that affect educational quality. This has especially damaged the public college and university systems that educate 75% of US college students. Funding reform will happen when a typical student uses Willie Sutton's line when asked why they went to the University of Chicago instead of the University of Illinois at Chicago: because that's where the money is.[37]

Tuition Sticker Price

Columbia University is one of the oldest and most storied institutions of higher learning in the United States. Columbia has joined most elite private universities in preserving its relatively small size despite tremendous growth in the US population. Columbia's 2,000-student graduating class in 2016 was 59% larger than its class in 1921. But the US population had tripled in size since the 1920s and the population of college-goers has increased by more than ten times.[1] As a result, high schoolers' demand to attend Columbia now far exceeds the university's capacity to educate them. In 2016, Columbia received more than 37,000 applications for fewer than 1,600 slots in its incoming freshman class.

While most private universities do not provide statistics about their applicants, the distribution of Columbia's student body is likely revealing about which students choose to apply and which do not. More than 60% of Columbia's students in the early 2000s came from the richest fifth of households in the United States—those whose income exceeds $110,000 per year. Meanwhile, just one in twenty Columbia students came from the bottom fifth of incomes—households whose income was less than $20,000 annually.[2] The median Columbia student's family income was $150,900, almost three times the nation's median household income at the time.[3]

Despite their small numbers, low-income students are served very well by Columbia. More than half of its graduates who were members

of the group with bottom-quintile family incomes when they were students had themselves moved to the top income quintile by the time
they reached their 30s, an impressive jump in socioeconomic mobility
matched by graduates of few other US universities. Given the small
number of working-class students at Columbia, however, this excellent
outcome matters for just 50 students each year. So why don't more low-
income students attend Columbia?

Aside from college admissions decisions (Ivy League universities
reject a large share of their lower-income applicants), another likely
explanation for the underrepresentation of lower-income students at
Columbia is that many of them never apply to the university. And a key
reason for that is the annual cost of attending Columbia. In May 2018,
when we Googled "Columbia tuition," the answer in Google's Knowledge Panel was an eye-popping $74,173 total cost (fig. 4.1). For a four-
year degree that's going to add up to $300,000. Who, you could imag-
ine many searchers wondering, can possibly pay this amount?

Maybe this is just Google, though. Does Columbia explain this price
better? Not at first. The 2022 "Facts and Figures" page on Columbia's
Financial Aid & Education Financing website, which appeared farther
down in the Google results, listed Columbia's $85,967 annual cost of
attendance, then listed additional costs, such as transcript and orien-
tation fees, that are not included in that amount before turning to a
short discussion of the actual price students pay for a Columbia education.[4] In its section on grants, it informs users that "Columbia awards
more than $200 million annually in scholarships and grants from all
sources" and that "50% of Columbia students receive grants from Columbia," but the actual cost of attending Columbia—or even just the
tuition price that families from different income levels could expect—
is never summarized. The only bullet point in the "Loans" section stated
that "students are expected to borrow $0 to attend Columbia," but the
prominent "Education Loans" tab on the top menu doesn't send the
same message.[5] A section titled "Income" claims that "parents with

FIGURE 4.1.

Google search results for "Columbia tuition"

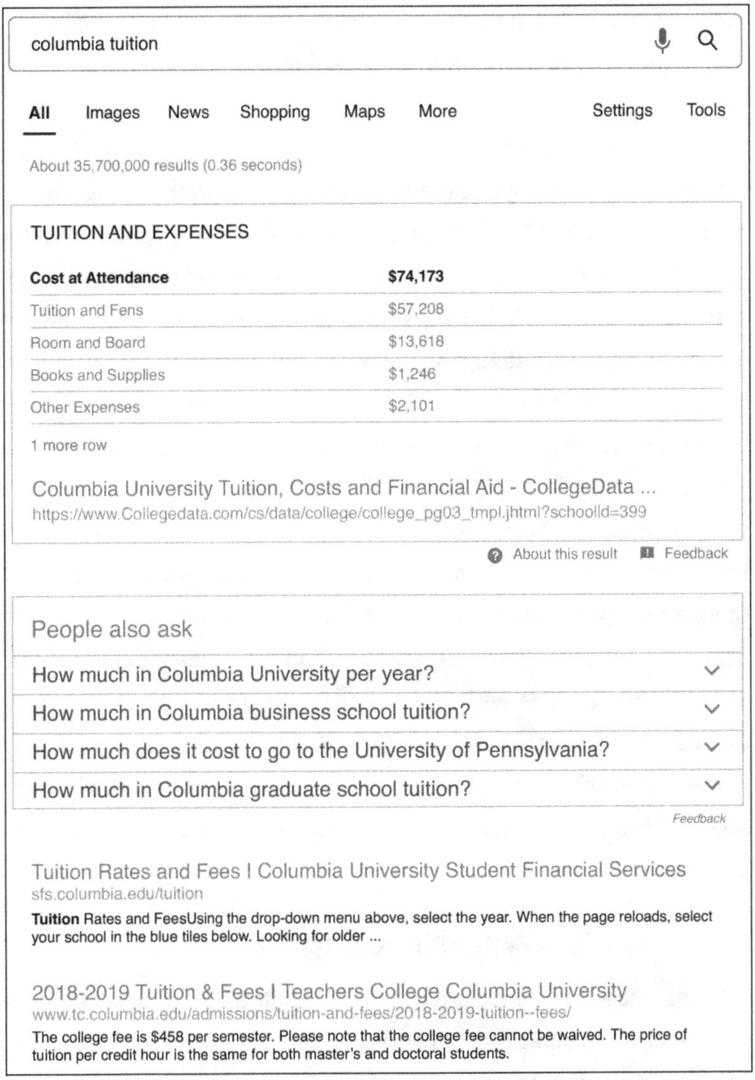

columbia tuition　　🎤　🔍

All　Images　News　Shopping　Maps　More　　　Settings　Tools

About 35,700,000 results (0.36 seconds)

TUITION AND EXPENSES

Cost at Attendance	$74,173
Tuition and Fens	$57,208
Room and Board	$13,618
Books and Supplies	$1,246
Other Expenses	$2,101

1 more row

Columbia University Tuition, Costs and Financial Aid - CollegeData ...
https://www.Collegedata.com/cs/data/college/college_pg03_tmpl.jhtml?schoolId=399

　　　　　　　　　　　　　　❓ About this result　　📓 Feedback

People also ask

How much in Columbia University per year?	⌄
How much in Columbia business school tuition?	⌄
How much does it cost to go to the University of Pennsylvania?	⌄
How much in Columbia graduate school tuition?	⌄

Feedback

Tuition Rates and Fees I Columbia University Student Financial Services
sfs.columbia.edu/tuition
Tuition Rates and FeesUsing the drop-down menu above, select the year. When the page reloads, select your school in the blue tiles below. Looking for older ...

2018-2019 Tuition & Fees I Teachers College Columbia University
www.tc.columbia.edu/admissions/tuition-and-fees/2018-2019-tuition--fees/
The college fee is $458 per semester. Please note that the college fee cannot be waived. The price of tuition per credit hour is the same for both master's and doctoral students.

calculated incomes below $66,000 a year and typical assets are expected to contribute $0 towards their children's Columbia education," but still we're left asking the real question: What would it actually cost such a student to attend Columbia University?

In fact, students from low-income households at Columbia pay nowhere near the astronomical prices presented by Google and Columbia's summary web page. And not half or even a quarter of it. According to data from the U.S. Department of Education, the average annual cost of Columbia room, board, and tuition for students from families with incomes from $30,000 to $48,000 was just $4,699.[6] That's roughly 5 cents out of every dollar of Columbia's publicized price. Even students with family incomes from $75,000 to $110,000 paid only $16,916 per year, which is less than the annual price of room and board in New York City alone; they paid essentially no tuition.

These actual prices of enrolling at Columbia University likely push its cost within reach of broad swaths of high school graduates. In fact, these annual net costs are lower than those of many New York public universities (SUNY Albany, for instance, had annual net prices of about $16,000 for families with around $40,000 of annual income and $21,000 for families with around $100,000 of annual income), let alone nearby private universities such as Pace University, which has annual net prices of $27,000 and $31,000 for the same two family income groups.[7]

Overestimating Costs

"Sticker prices" are far removed from the information most students need in order to make carefully considered decisions about which university to attend. In fact, at Columbia and other universities across the country, advertised sticker prices merely reflect the *maximum* cost students could face and many students ultimately pay steeply discounted prices. In addition to failing to reflect available federal and state grants or institutional discounts, sticker prices don't capture meaningful differences in students' living situations (e.g., students would pay less if they lived at home). At the same time, they ignore the fact that prices rise annually: by the time a student graduates, their maximum annual cost may be much higher than it was the year they started. But most important, sticker prices show university cost estimates that far exceed the true costs of attendance for most students.

Despite these flaws, sticker prices are prominently emblazoned on most university websites and are frequently discussed in the news media and by politicians. Go to the website of *U.S. News & World Report*'s "National University Rankings" and you'll find the sticker price of tuition listed for each ranked university.[8] Popular college ranking websites by the *Times Higher Education* and *Forbes* also highlight sticker prices, although *Forbes* also includes some information about financial aid.[9]

This prominent placement of a misleading indicator is not only unhelpful to potential college students and their families, it also confuses them about the actual cost of attending college. Sticker prices that imply that attending college for four years costs of hundreds of thousands of dollars can easily discourage even upper-middle-income families from sending their children to their preferred college and may discourage lower-income high school graduates from applying altogether. The problem is most acute for students without sources of accurate information about college costs, like those whose parents didn't go to college or who attend a high school with too few college counselors or with counselors who aren't knowledgeable enough to help them. By discouraging such students from attending college or from attending elite and private colleges that often advertise the highest sticker prices, this indicator may exacerbate income disparities by falsely inflating the expected cost of university attendance for lower-income students.

In January 2015, one of our authors (Zachary Bleemer) and a colleague tested this hypothesis by conducting a nationwide survey assessing the accuracy of adults' beliefs about the cost of college attendance.[10] After collecting demographic and other baseline information from each respondent, we asked them the following four questions:

> **Sticker** cost is a college's published cost of attendance. The cost of attendance includes tuition, fees and housing as well as other important costs like books, supplies and transportation. What is your best guess of the current average annual sticker cost of a 4-year Bachelor's degree at a: Public university? ____ Nonprofit private university? ____
>
> Many students who go to college qualify for grants and scholarships (money that students get that they don't have to work for or pay back), and as a result end up paying less than the sticker cost. This cost of college after taking into account grants and scholarships is referred to as the **net** college cost. This is the amount that students actually have to pay. What is your best guess of the current average annual net cost of a 4-year Bachelor's degree at a: Public university? ____ Nonprofit private university? ____

We then compared respondents' answers to actual average college costs in the most recent completed academic year, 2013–2014.

Table 4.1 summarizes our initial findings. The sticker prices of public universities (which are directly subsidized by state governments) were much lower than those of nonprofit private universities, but they were still high. Public universities advertised average sticker prices of just over $18,000 per year, while the private schools advertised an average price of about $41,000.[11] Net prices, however, were far lower. Students at public universities received government and institutional grants that averaged about $5,500, bringing their average annual net cost to $12,500, or a discount of 31%. Students at private institutions were offered an average of $17,500 in grant aid. So their average net price was $23,500, or a discount of 43%. Remember, these net prices

TABLE 4.1.

Actual and perceived average college prices in 2015 among a national sample of US adults

AVERAGE US COST OF COLLEGE	ACTUAL PRICE ($)	PERCEIVED PRICE ($)	AVERAGE ERROR (%)
Public university sticker price	18,400	30,600	+66
Public university net price	12,600	23,300	+85
Private university sticker price	40,900	43,400	+6
Private university net price	23,300	35,200	+51

Source: Zachary Bleemer and Basit Zafar, "Intended College Attendance: Evidence from an Experiment on College Returns and Costs," *Journal of Public Economics* 157 (2018): 184–211.

are the *average* prices students pay at public and private universities; students from lower-income backgrounds paid even lower prices.

The results from our survey suggested that most US adults had relatively good information about the sticker prices of private universities: their average estimate was $43,400, just 6% over the actual number.[12] But most adults greatly overestimated the cost of attending a four-year public university and the *net* cost of attending a nonprofit private university. Survey participants estimated that the average sticker price for public schools was almost $31,000, about 66% higher than the true average sticker price, and they thought that the average net cost at those schools was over $23,000, almost double the true number. The average estimate of the net costs of attending a private university, $35,200, was too high by about $12,000 per year. Overall, our survey respondents were almost twice as likely to overestimate the cost of public university enrollment as they were to underestimate it.

Why did the survey participants get these numbers so wrong? We thought that maybe people were more attuned to the prices of local universities than they are to national averages, but when we compared our survey respondents' estimates to the costs of nearby colleges, we found that respondents who lived near lower-cost universities were no less likely to overestimate college costs than those who lived near more expensive universities. Another potential explanation is what economists call "rational ignorance"—maybe only people who are making decisions about attending college, for example college-age students and their parents, need to pay attention to college costs—but what we found was that as young people approach college age, their parents' overestimation of the cost of higher education increases.

A third possible explanation is that survey participants may have over-extrapolated from the rising cost of higher education and believed that net costs are increasing faster than they are. But all of those stories about enormous tuition inflation are about sticker prices, not the prices that most students actually pay to go to college. In fact, the average net tuition and fees at both public and private universities didn't change at all in the period 2006 to 2020 after adjusting for inflation. That is because the amount of grants and other discounts increased at the same rate as the sticker prices of universities.[13] Once again, the underlying explanation for this misperception seems to be the proliferation of information about the high sticker prices of private universities.

Let's go back to our survey. To better understand the role of sticker price information in how people make decisions about attending college, we asked our survey respondents whether they had children. If they did, we asked them the following question about their oldest child below the age of 18: "If this child were to attend college, what do you think the annual net college cost (the cost that the child and/or the family will actually have to pay) would be? Please ignore the effects of inflation."

Once again, respondents substantially overestimated the cost of attending a university, this time for their own children. Because about 70% of university students attend in-state public universities, the average net cost of attending any university in 2013 was just under $16,000. Even though our respondents were representative of the US population, their average estimate of the cost of attending university for their own children was more than $25,000. More surprisingly, despite the fact that lower-income families tend to have lower university costs than higher-income families—both because students from such families are more likely to attend public universities and because they tend to receive greater financial aid—we found no evidence that lower-income respondents expected lower university costs for their children than higher-income respondents. Moreover, the higher each respondent believed average private sticker prices to be, the more expensive they thought college would be for their own children. Every $1,000 increase in a respondent's belief about average private sticker prices was associated with a $300 increase in what they expected their own child to pay for attending college. Altogether, this evidence suggests that most people significantly overestimate the cost of college for their own children and that the prevalence of sticker prices drives these overestimates.

We ran one additional test to confirm our hypothesis that people who overestimate average college costs also overestimate what they think college will cost for their own children. At the end of our survey, we randomly split the respondents into a treatment group and a control group. We reminded the control group of their beliefs about average net costs but didn't give them any additional information. But we gave the treatment group accurate information about the net cost of attending college:

> Earlier in the survey we had asked you about college net costs. This is the cost of college after taking into account grants and scholarships (money that students get that they don't have to work for or pay back), and is the price that students actually have to pay. In many cases, this is less than the published college cost (the sticker cost).
>
> You had stated that you expect the average annual net cost of a Bachelor's degree at a 4-year public university to be _____ and at a 4-year nonprofit private university to be _____.

According to the College Board Annual Survey of Colleges, the average annual net cost of a 4-year public university in 2013–2014 was $12,620, while that of a 4-year nonprofit private university was $23,290.

After letting that sink in, we asked respondents in both groups to update their beliefs about the cost of college for their own children. Did they still think that their previous response was reasonable?

For many people in the treatment group, the answer was no: after people learned what college actually costs for the average US household, they changed their beliefs of what college would cost for their own children. Take a parent who guessed that the average net cost of enrolling at a public university was about $23,000 per year—about $10,000 higher than the true amount—and who thought that their own child's expected college costs would be about $25,000. After hearing about what college actually costs for most people, parents revised their estimate of what college would cost their own child to less than $22,000 per year.

These survey results have a clear interpretation. While widely available sticker prices have led many families to overestimate the cost of attending college, providing simple statistics such as the average net prices college students and their families pay can help people adjust their expectations and better understand what college would actually cost them. For some families, maybe that change would have been enough to make the difference.

The Cost of Overestimating Cost

What harm is done when people overestimate university costs? Does this overestimation matter for any practical purposes, especially because it seems to affect both lower-income and higher-income families?

The most obvious effect is that people may be less likely to attend college themselves or may be more likely to recommend against attending college when they talk to their children or friends. Misinformation spreads easily—especially in the form of indicators like sticker prices that are easy to misinterpret—and perceived higher prices tend to dissuade people from almost all purchases or investments, including attending college. When people decide not to go to college because of inaccurate perceptions of the cost, they miss out on the personal benefits of higher education and all of us lose the benefits to society that accrue from more highly educated communities.

Overestimating college costs likely also impacts the kinds of universities that students apply to and attend, especially those from lower-income families. Despite the fact that many private universities are actually cheaper to attend than nearby public universities for lower-income students because of generous financial aid, the large gap between the sticker prices of selective private and public universities likely pushes many lower-income students to attend the latter, even if the student believes that the former would offer a higher-quality education.[14] The same is likely true for students from families or communities where few people went to college because information about the value of college education is more difficult for them to obtain. At the national scale, these forces may tend to push lower-income students out of the country's highest-quality universities.

Finally, overestimating college costs almost surely damages the reputation of universities as accessible institutions that promote socioeconomic mobility, especially for public universities. As the skyrocketing sticker prices of private universities have generated misinformation about the cost of attending public institutions, voters seem to have cooled toward the public funding of universities, increasingly perceiving them as bastions for higher-income students.[15] These sentiments ironically have led state legislatures to decrease their annual investment in public universities, which in turn has led universities to charge higher tuition.

Interestingly, the empirical evidence about the ramifications of the widespread overestimation of college costs in the United States is relatively thin. Unfortunately, despite (or perhaps because of) wide agreement that overestimates of college costs would actively dissuade some young people from attending college, very few studies have directly tested this theory.[16] In 2013, economists Caroline Hoxby and Sarah Turner published a study about the second potential effect—that overestimating college costs discourages lower-income students from attending higher-quality universities. They conducted a large-scale experiment among high-achieving, low-income high school students across the United States in 2011.[17] Hoxby and Turner randomly divided a large group of such students into treatment and control groups and mailed the treatment group a packet of detailed information about the annual net cost of attending a variety of both nearby and nationwide universities. They presented this information as the average cost for families at three income levels—$20,000, $40,000, and $60,000—so that students could extrapolate their own expected costs if they were to attend each university. In a second experiment, the same information was mailed directly to students' parents, this time including additional details about the graduation rates and average wages of graduates from each university.

Hoxby and Turner's key finding is that students in both of these treatment groups (the one in which students received information and the other in which parents received information) applied to more and better universities than those in the control group and were more likely to be admitted to better universities, which the researchers categorized based on average SAT scores and graduation rates. Not all of these students actually attended better universities as a result, although those whose parents received the information about net costs were somewhat more likely to do so. They also found that when application fees were waived, these effects were greatly magnified.

The study results suggest that lower-income students' overestimation of university costs warps their decisions about which colleges to apply to and that the simple intervention of giving college students and their families information about the true cost of attending college can meaningfully improve their decisions. This was an exciting finding, and in 2016 the College Board tried to replicate it on a massive scale. It mailed detailed information, including average net college costs for lower- and middle-income households, to hundreds of thousands of lower-income students who took the SAT exam. Unfortunately, this time the mailers had no effect on which universities the students in the treatment group chose to attend.[18] Maybe students didn't read the information from the College Board or maybe they didn't trust the information that it provided. Either way, it seems that cookie-cutter informational mailers aren't a magic bullet; widespread misinformation about college costs will have to be combated using other tools.

It would be better if prospective college students had access to easy-to-use, interactive, and personalized net cost information for all the universities they wanted to apply to. Fortunately, one such indicator already exists for many universities and seems to be slowly proliferating.

MyinTuition: A Replacement for Sticker Price Data

As a result of a federal mandate in the Higher Education Opportunity Act of 2008, most US universities have added financial aid calculators to their websites that function as a sort of pre-application estimator of what students can expect to pay for a year of college.[19] Prospective students can type in a large amount of information about their family's finances—a process that typically takes about 20 minutes—and receive a net-cost estimate for attending that university.

While these first-generation cost calculators are a substantial improvement over only advertising sticker prices, they have a number of

FIGURE 4.2.

Initial page of the MyinTuition financial aid calculator for Amherst College

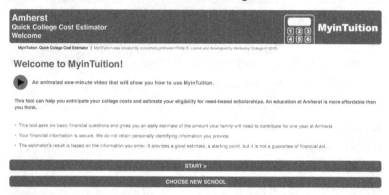

Source: https://myintuition.org/quick-college-cost-estimator/.

shortcomings. They are not integrated across universities, which means that it can be very time consuming for students to compare their expected net costs across many universities and they require students to know and provide very detailed information about their family's financial state. They also differ substantially from school to school, making them somewhat difficult to use.

A second generation of cost calculators are just starting to appear that have made important improvements over the tools on university websites. A great example is a simplified and streamlined financial aid calculator called MyinTuition (fig. 4.2) that was developed by economist Phillip Levine. It was first released at Wellesley College in 2013 and by 2021 it was available for seventy-one colleges and universities. Championed by *New York Times* columnist David Leonhart since its inception, the tool asks participants just seven questions about their family income and living situation.[20] You can see the questions in table 4.2.

From the answers to these questions, the tool generates the expected cost of attending the university the user has selected and a low

TABLE 4.2.

Financial aid questions asked in the MyinTuition app

1. What is your citizenship status? What is your current living situation (that is, how many of your parents are you living with)?

2. What is your family's total annual income before taxes?

3. Does your family own the home in which you live? If so, what is the current value of the family's home? What is the remaining balance on your mortgage?

4. Do your parents have any cash held in a regular savings or checking account? If so, what is the total cash balance in these accounts?

5. Do your parents have any retirement or pension plans? If yes, what is the value of those retirement plans?

6. Do your parents have any investments held in non-retirement accounts? If yes, what is the value of those non-retirement investments?

7. Do you have any siblings who will also be enrolled full time in a four-year undergraduate institution in the same year that you plan to enter college? If so, how many siblings will be enrolled?

Source: MyinTuition, "Quick College Cost Estimator," https://myintuition.org/quick-college -cost-estimator/.

and high price designed to illustrate the range of possible costs a student would incur (depending on other factors not captured by the seven questions, especially merit-based aid). Users can easily change their answers—e.g., increasing the expected number of siblings who will simultaneously be enrolled at college, which may give a better sense of a students' future net costs if their siblings enroll in college— to see how the net costs of attending a particular university would change given different family circumstances. They can also save their financial information and apply it to any of the other participating institutions, making it easy to compare personalized net costs across a variety of colleges and universities.

MyinTuition is mostly available for private universities; only a handful of public universities participate. Whether more universities adopt the platform or develop their own second-generation net cost calculators, providing quick, personalized information about the net cost of attending a particular university to interested applicants is likely an important way to improve public knowledge about universities and broaden access to university education. Indeed, an early study of the impact of MyinTuition shows that the tool has substantially increased application rates among students for whom it was available.[21]

Second-generation net cost calculators offer an unusually high bar for university indicators. They are easy to use and carefully targeted to their intended user group of parents and high school students. They provide personalized information for students from different backgrounds and their interactive interfaces enable students to see how college costs would adapt to changes in their family's financial situation. They present best- and worst-case scenarios for users, margins of error that help students and their parents to evaluate the risks of potentially facing higher college costs than a single cost estimate would suggest. Second-generation financial aid calculators sometimes provide links to universities' first-generation financial aid calculators for students who are willing to provide more information and time in return for more detailed cost estimates. Most important, they do not present themselves as the all-encompassing basis of any student's decision about which college to attend. Instead, they present accurate information that can be usefully integrated into the decisions families make about which college a student might apply to.

In short, the personalized information second-generation net cost calculators such as MyinTuition provide is a strong alternative to the sticker prices universities currently broadcast, providing a broader range of helpful information while correcting the overestimated beliefs about the cost of a college education that many people in the United States have.

Conclusion

Students pay wildly different costs to attend the same college, depending mainly on their financial circumstances. Sticker prices reflect college costs that only fairly affluent students can expect to pay and are not relevant for most students. Their widespread availability leads to serious overestimations of college costs that impact decisions about which colleges to apply to and about university education as a value proposition.

Second-generation net cost calculators such as MyinTuition aren't the only possible improvement on sticker prices. For example, net cost information by family income level is now accessible for all U.S. colleges and universities on the federal College Scorecard website and through other organizations.[22] A recent study from the University of Michigan showed that guaranteeing lower income students' financial aid packages even before they choose whether to send in an application led to large increases in application rates and enrollment. This strategy merges the idea of cost calculators with students' actual financial aid awards in a way that clearly simplifies students' decision-making.[23]

Metrics and informational tools that help correct misperceptions about the high cost of college education—which are especially prevalent among families with parents who did not attend college and lower-income families—are important steps forward. These false beliefs affect all of us by reducing the social benefits of having a larger population of college-educated people, inhibiting socioeconomic mobility, and unnecessarily damaging the reputation of colleges and universities. They are perpetuated by an indicator that masquerades as the price of attending college when in fact it merely reflects a college's maximum price, one that is paid primarily by high-income families who do not receive discounts from the federal government, the state, the institution, or other organizations. The net cost of attending an institution is and should be a crucial component of the decisions families make about which colleges students should apply to. While sticker prices are easy to obtain, they are a highly inaccurate proxy for net cost data.

Sticker prices seem to already have some momentum working against them, led by the journalist David Leonhart, the Urban Institute's Understanding College Affordability team, and others.[24] We mentioned at the beginning of the chapter that in 2018, a Google search of "Columbia tuition" provided only information about Columbia University's sticker price. By the spring of 2021, Google's top response still highlighted Columbia's sticker price for tuition, but in a smaller font halfway down the page Google also listed Columbia's "average cost after aid" and additional financial aid information was available toward the bottom of the page. While there is clearly much more progress to be made, we are hopeful that the end of the widespread dissemination of sticker prices is near. Students and their families can play a crucial role in this reform by looking beyond sticker prices as they make their choices.

Scorekeeping Student Debt

If you're reading this book, you're likely already familiar with the problem of expanding, even exploding, student debt. It has ballooned to $1.5 trillion, it has increased more than sixfold since 2003, and it now makes up 11% of all household debt in the United States.[1] But behind these numbers lies something far more pernicious. This debt is at the center of a transformation of higher education into something no one really wants. It now produces a sea of indebted, wage-obsessed graduates, a far cry from its original mission of producing an informed or even enlightened public that is well prepared to tackle the problems of today's and tomorrow's society, economy, and democracy.[2]

There is now widespread—although far from universal—criticism of this method of funding higher education. Initially led by radical organizations like Strike Debt!, the movement against student debt has moved into the mainstream of US politics.[3] There is momentum in the Democratic Party for significant reforms, such as abandoning public university tuition and forgiving student debt.[4] Despite this, the federal government has pushed us farther down the path of imagining higher education in strictly financial terms. One of the government's most important interventions in the higher education system in the last decade is the creation of the College Scorecard, which compares and evaluates every college and university in overly simplistic financial terms. Those who celebrate the scorecard argue that it promotes transparency that encourages prospective students to make objective choices. But as we show below, at best the scorecard provides flawed information that is misleading and removed from essential context. Perhaps more important, the scorecard encourages everyone involved to think about higher education as a commodity that is purchased in a private market transaction.

At the most basic level, debt reduces a student's future into one determined by the number of dollars they owe. One of the mottos of Strike Debt! is "you are not a loan," but unless and until the current system of funding higher education is radically changed, the everyday lives of many students, former students, and parents will be deeply influenced by the amount of money they owe. If a former student fails to pay down their debt in a timely fashion, their future—which is a kind of collateral for the loan—can be wrecked with late fees, garnished wages, and a ruined credit score. Furthermore, students face the loss of freedom to choose an education and career that fits best with who they are or who they want to be.

This is one of the great ironies of relying on student loans as a funding model.[5] The historical role of US higher education has been to open up the futures of students—to encourage them to create new relationships, freely pursue their ambition, and develop adaptability to cope with a quickly changing world. But with financial calculation now at the forefront, higher education is doing the opposite. Student debt closes off possible futures, not least by discouraging students from embarking on lower-wage careers that may be individually rewarding or highly valuable to society. Some students certainly value high wages above other pursuits, but what about those who want to pursue careers in teaching, social work, environmental advocacy, or art? The implication of many of the financial metrics now used to assess the value of college is that you would be unwise (or at least be taking great financial risks) if you used debt to pay for a university education that leads to these careers.[6] But what if student loans are your only option?

In light of these questions, the message of this chapter is relatively simple. Student loans are complicated and hugely consequential and must be taken seriously by every prospective student. But we encourage you to avoid falling into the trap of thinking that the main purpose of universities is to produce wages. The decision of how to finance a university education is deeply personal, and given that 70% of college graduates carry some student debt, you will very likely be impacted by it. We cannot offer a magic bullet metric that will tell you the optimal level of debt. This chapter is meant to help you understand some of the recent history of student debt, why the growth in that debt has encouraged the proliferation of financial metrics, and how both of these are contributing to an environment where it may seem like your only choice is to pursue a high-wage career.

A Short History of Student Debt

The conversation about student loan policies in the United States is increasingly complicated. Most students now borrow from the same places, but borrowers can end up in a variety of repayment plans. More and more, they are now in some kind of income-driven repayment program. Originally designed to make sure that borrowers don't face a preposterous monthly bill, these programs now amount to a sort of tax.[7] In these plans, borrowers may make payments for decades, never fully paying the loan off, and then after a set period, the government will "generously" cancel what remains. Regardless of your repayment plan, debt transactions are at the heart of university life today, and because of that, there is now a necessary link between universities and Wall Street.

For lenders, student loans are a liability. Unlike most other types of loans, with a student loan, no collateral can be repossessed if the borrower stops paying. In place of a physical asset, students' futures have become collateral, something to be tracked, surveilled, threatened, and risk managed. Because in this way of thinking universities are charging a fee to improve students' financial futures and because the federal government provides the upfront funding for tuition through student loans, the government encourages universities to behave in ways that maximize the chance that each student can fully and speedily repay their debt.[8] One form that this accountability takes is widely available money-related metrics such as the average debt statistics on the College Scorecard and estimates of future wages and return on investment.[9]

There is a rationality to this system, but it comes with costs. As student debt increasingly becomes the primary funding source for universities, the usual reaction is to judge the success of universities by standardized metrics related to how students will pay off those loans. Yet, as the philosopher Michael Sandel explains, judging things in strictly monetary terms has a tendency to change the things being judged, oftentimes in ways that most people do not want.[10] In the case of public universities, relying on student debt as the primary funding mechanism is making it increasingly difficult for them to serve any sort of common cause or public good unless that too is justified in financial terms.

Before we get too far, let's consider why there has been such a dramatic increase in student debt. It must be rising tuition costs, right? On the surface, this makes sense, but the causal relationship is not quite right. In fact, scholars across several disciplines have demonstrated that increases in tuition at many public universities were possible only because US state legislatures and university administrators knew that increasing amounts of government-backed credit was available to students.[11] At a minimum, if the credit available to students had been more limited, the decision to raise tuition would have been more difficult because it might have decreased the number of students able to pay. We are not suggesting that credit should be limited; what we are saying is that its availability has served as a rationale for policymakers and college administrators to raise tuition fees.

SCOREKEEPING STUDENT DEBT **75**

Questions about the necessity of student loans are relatively new. Higher education in the United States was not always funded through high tuition. From the late nineteenth century to the 1980s, public university tuition was typically quite low, there was little need for student loans, and federal subsidies mostly took the form of grants.[12] Perhaps the most famous federal subsidy is the 1944 Servicemen's Readjustment Act, popularly known as the GI Bill, which covered most if not all college expenses for World War II veterans. A generation later, as part of President Lyndon B. Johnson's Great Society initiatives, Congress passed the 1965 Higher Education Act, which allowed for government-guaranteed student loans and was a broad attempt to expand access to higher education to those who might be excluded for financial reasons. When he signed the bill, Johnson said, "It means that a high school senior anywhere in this great land of ours can apply to any college or any university in any of the 50 States and not be turned away because his family is poor."[13] Things have changed quite a lot since then. You might not be turned away, but many are frightened away from many public universities because of the prospects of indebtedness.

In 1972, Congress reauthorized the Higher Education Act and created a new federal agency, the Student Loan Marketing Association, or Sallie Mae, to expand the private market for federally backed student loans. Sallie Mae accomplished this by buying up individual loans from private banks, bundling them, and then selling the bundles to investors. This had the effect of growing the market for student loans, but it took until the 1990s for private banks to recognize the immense profit opportunities from issuing low-risk, federally insured private loans.

Not everyone liked the idea of private banks profiting just for facilitating what had begun as part of President Johnson's Great Society initiative, which in large part was an attempt to alleviate poverty. Critics argued that the federal government could save $1 billion per year by directly issuing loans to students.[14] So when the quantity of these loans began to grow significantly in the early 1990s, President Bill Clinton wanted the federal government to sidestep private banks and offer loans directly to students. The Republican Congress resisted this move, and in 1994 a compromise was reached whereby the federal government was allowed to offer loans directly to students but in exchange Sallie Mae was privatized and allowed to issue both government-insured loans and private uninsured loans directly to students.

This was the true beginning of the establishment of what has been aptly called the "student finance complex."[15] For the financial industry, the student loan business became very lucrative. In the period 2010 to 2013, for example, Sallie Mae earned $3.5 billion, and between 1995 and 2005, its stock price rose by 1,900%.[16] At the same time, in the period 1997 to 2016, Sallie Mae spent $44 million lobbying Congress to protect its privileged position as a private provider of government-backed loans.[17]

These changes caused huge increases in the amount of credit available to students. University administrators saw this as an opportunity to raise tuition and a decreasing need to fight for general revenues from the public purse. This resulted in a significant change in the source of funding for public universities. In inflation-adjusted terms, in the period 1976 to 2010, average in-state tuition at four-year US institutions roughly tripled, from $2,524 to $7,618 in 2013 dollars. In 1975, US states contributed an average of 58% of the costs of public higher education, but by 2016, that number had dropped to 37%.[18] Analyzing U.S. Bureau of Economic Analysis data, reporters James Steele and Lance Williams estimate that this reduction in states' contributions is worth $500 billion. Much of this gap was funded by tuition increases, which in turn necessitated increasing student indebtedness. The bottom line is that there has been a significant change in the way public higher education is funded in the United States over the last forty years.

How did this happen? One explanation is that since 1980 there has been a paradigm shift in how economists, politicians, and large parts of the public think about public higher education. Instead of imagining students as members of a public with shared democratic and socioeconomic goals, the post-1980 paradigm sees them as private beneficiaries of increased future wages. Put differently, this is more than just a shift in the way higher education is paid for. The move to fund public universities through private tuition is slowly but surely evacuating the public spirit from higher education. Instead of a set of social institutions that produce public goods, many policymakers now see universities as economic institutions that above all else produce *private goods*.

We should not, however, look at this in completely cynical terms. During this period there was also a significant increase in socioeconomic inequality. This meant that although the risks of ending up with a low-wage job increased, the rewards of ending up with a high-wage job also increased. Salaries at the very top exploded, even as the chance of attaining those top-paying jobs decreased. In other words, the job market became more like a lottery with lots of losers and a few dramatic winners. Why would taxpayers choose to buy lottery tickets for everyone when so few would win?[19] Furthermore, why bother when the dominant ideology suggests that the poor should use the available credit to buy their own ticket? Of course reasonable people disagree about this, but we think this is shortsighted vision and that it is an effect of narrowly imagining higher education as a purely economic good instead of one with much wider benefits.

In this system of thought, individual human capital takes precedence over public goods. For the proponents of this new paradigm, it makes complete sense that the beneficiaries of these private goods should pay for them in tuition, whether up front or over time in the form of loans. Even when loans are subsidized by the federal government and even though they flow through universities, it is individual students who are ultimately responsible for repaying the debt. Thus, these loans more closely resemble private market transactions than public investments.

The private nature of higher education has been intensified by the almost complete prohibition on discharging student debt through bankruptcy proceedings. This process began in 1975, when both private banks and Congress became increasingly uneasy with student loan default. During the 1970s and into the 1980s, there was widespread criticism of spendthrift "student deadbeats" who were accused of taking advantage of federally subsidized credit, then recklessly declaring bankruptcy and wiping their debt clean shortly after finishing school.[20] Through a series of changes to federal laws, student loan debt was made nondischargeable except in extreme circumstances. As a result, canceling student loan debt by declaring bankruptcy is now nearly impossible. This helps explain why a shocking number of those over 65 years old in the United States are still encumbered by student loans and has resulted in the perverse situation where the federal government garnished retirees' Social Security checks to the tune of $150 million in 2013 alone. Some of these retirees might be carrying their children's student debt, but regardless, the Government Accountability Office reports that from 2002 to 2013, the number of people over 65 who lost part of their Social Security payments to pay off federal student loans increased by 400%.[21] We appreciate that every individual circumstance is unique, but can anyone reasonably argue that this arrangement reflects the public spirit of higher education?

Over time, the vision of privatized public higher education has become common sense for many on both the political right and left. The Obama administration ended the practice of outsourcing federally subsidized student loans to private lenders in 2010, which removed one financial influence from universities. But another of President Obama's interventions was the creation of the College Scorecard. Obama recognized that the explosion in student debt was a problem, but instead of pushing for debt forgiveness or for funding increases for public universities, his administration chose to provide students with "better" information about college financing. The U.S. Department of Education created a new website where it collected and published comparative data on the costs of college, average debt accrued, and future wages of students at thousands of US higher education institutions.

The resulting College Scorecard was launched in 2015. Despite Obama's early insistence that the scorecard rank colleges by their costs or average debt, it does not do so because of the fierce resistance of many college and university presidents. Instead, it enables users to compare different universities in an unranked list. Even without the ranking, the idea was that universities would be forced to compete with each other in an information-rich pseudo-market for college debt. The assumption was that colleges and universities would be incentivized to lower their costs and improve their "products" or suffer the loss of "customers." So while Obama recognized the burden of the immense growth in debt and took some steps to alleviate it, an important part of his solution was to reinforce the vision of university education as an individual investment in the potential for future wages.[22] In this scheme, higher education as a whole is mostly reduced to a simple financial metric.

The Secretary of Education in the Trump administration, Betsy DeVos, continued to emphasize the importance of the College Scorecard. At the end of 2019, the Department of Education rolled out an updated version of it that enabled potential students to compare degree programs in terms of costs, debt incurred, and future wages. So in addition to comparing New York University to CUNY Hunter College to SUNY Buffalo, a potential student can now compare the same data for a bachelor's degree in urban studies at these schools. In the press release rolling out this new feature, DeVos emphasized the importance of "transparency," saying that it "ensures students can make apples-to-apples comparisons by providing the same data about all of the programs a student might be considering without regard to the type of school."[23] The idea that the federal government will help universities provide clear information is a good one. But the problem comes in treating every college and university as "apples"—a simple consumer good with easily defined quality—when in reality universities are multidimensional and serve many different functions for different students. In effect, this metric reduces universities and their degree programs to knowledge economy factories in which students are the inputs on one end of the assembly line and future wages minus debts are the outputs at the other end.

We will discuss the many flaws in the College Scorecard data in greater detail in the next chapter. We have no quarrel with the federal government and universities offering transparency. The problem comes when this transparency is used as a justification for the production of an imaginary marketplace in which every college and every student is equal and the public sees the function of universities as limited to selling private goods to consumers. This shift from public to private higher education is damaging US democracy.[24] It has contributed to the delegitimization of the idea that a society can make the collective choice to educate its citizenry and pay for it with collective taxes. And it has devalued the kind of liberal arts education necessary for maintaining a public capacity to understand complex political-economic problems and cultural shifts or to use the lessons of history to analyze them.[25]

Rethinking the Bonds of Debt

Despite what we have said, there is nothing inherently malign or corrupting about debt. Borrowing money can be a simple and straightforward short-term convenience. Examples include a credit card that you pay off at the end of a month or loans that enable people to buy assets that they cannot pay for in a lump sum. There is also nothing inherently positive about debt. What matters is the kind of debt, who controls it, and what happens when debts are not repaid. Most important in this case, student debt is not just a way to pay tuition. As social scientists and philosophers have been pointing out for decades, debt is just a form of social obligation, and these obligations are one of the basic ways that societies are held together (and torn apart when they are not met). What we find troubling is that the weight of monetary obligations in higher education are crowding out other obligations related to critical thinking and democratic citizenship. This is the problem with the College Scorecard. It does a good job of comparing universities in simple monetary terms, but it is not a good way to make sense of what kind of actual experience you will have when you enroll at one of them. It is also not a useful way to understand the value of colleges and a college education to public life.

When a person takes out a student loan, they do not owe the government an education in return. Instead, they just owe a quantity of dollars. This simplifies things, but it also encourages us to compare many things with a single quantitative metric—money. This quantification enables the transformation of a complicated set of educational obligations into "a matter of impersonal arithmetic."[26] At the same time, this arithmetic has become the basis of the bonds between universities, governments, and the financial sector, which draws on the full force of law to ensure that former students and their families repay. Even while it cultivates a middle-class ethic of financial planning and responsibility, the machinery of the "student finance complex" is not designed to take into account the personal lives and circumstances of individual students and their families.[27] There are of course exceptions, but for the most part this complex is an indifferent tracking system enabled by Social Security numbers and credit ratings. These ratings are now used to assess much more than how likely you are to pay back a debt. They have become a general measurement of social trustworthiness. A bad credit rating can keep you from getting a home or a job. Credit ratings are regularly used to assess home-rental applications and they are also routinely used to assess job applicants, although the latter practice is illegal in eleven states.[28] Failure to make payments on student loans could mean vicious cycles of reduced employment quality and lowered credit quality.

It is difficult to deny that these new bonds between the financial sector, universities, and students are drifting toward immorality.[29] For the financial sector, student debt has become a basis of wealth accumulation. Private-sector creditors in particular seek out students with higher risk profiles because they are more likely to agree to loans with higher interest rates that are potentially more profitable—assuming the borrowers do not default. Borrowers of these "subprime" student loans are more apt to be poor and/or racial and ethnic minorities, making the student loan "economy" discriminatory in some of the same ways as the home mortgage industry of the late 1990s and the 2000s.[30] If enrolling in college is no more than a simple financial transaction, perhaps these relationships with the banking sector are entirely moral. But we think college is about much more than this.

The crucial point is that the long-term shift from public funding to student debt has had a privatizing effect. That is, instead of a mutual and public obligation between society (to fund institutions of higher learning) and students (to take on the responsibilities of citizenship), we now have a system in which individual students enter into an economic transaction with universities to buy the capacity to earn greater wages in the future. Earning higher wages was certainly not ignored in the past. But it was a subordinate concern and a side effect of producing an educated citizenry. If we evaluate universities only in financial terms, universities have fewer obligations to serve the broader public (at least as anything other than an aggregate of individual economic interests) and the broader public has fewer incentives to fund universities. As numerous scholars have pointed out, the high-tuition/high-debt model intensifies declining public support for public universities, which then makes it easier to justify higher tuition rather than tax-payer funding.[31] To put this differently, the complex qualitative obligations between universities and the public are being weakened at the same time that quantitative financial obligations between students, universities, and the financial sector are being strengthened.

Financial metrics such as return on investment, wages by major, and many aspects of the College Scorecard are playing a central role in this shift. The scorecard is doing much more than keeping score. It is touted as a simple metric that encourages transparency, but it is built on all sorts of assumptions, including that a college education is just a means to the end of increasing wages in the future. In other words, the model on which the scorecard is built assumes that college is primarily a financial investment whose rewards will exclusively benefit the buyer rather than the public.

Conclusion

Whether college is worth it and especially whether you should take on debt to pay for college are deeply personal questions. The answers to them are highly dependent on your circumstances. The real message of this chapter, however, is not about whether or not you ought to take on debt and how much debt you should incur. Rather, the message is that going to college is about more than money. In fact, it is about more than just you. Of course higher education will improve your life, but it will also benefit society, economy, and democracy. And because of this, several things are clear: as many people as possible should go to college, the public should put more effort into making college accessible to everyone who wants to attend, and we should stop doing that through a financial tradeoff that in some cases lasts through retirement.

The quantitative metrics that have emerged in the last twenty years to make sense of higher education cannot tell us much about democratic governance, public life, or the common good. Metrics such as return on investment, which companies such as PayScale promote explicitly and the federal government promotes implicitly through its College Score-card, are capable only of characterizing the costs and benefits of higher education for individual students and only in terms of money. With 1.5 trillion dollars' worth of individual students' social obligations circulating through our society, no one should be surprised that students, families, universities, and governments are relatively obsessed with metrics that explain whether and how those obligations will be met. In this environment, we would never advise you to ignore them. But you should also be aware that in many instances, these metrics are providing you with incomplete information.

The logic behind the College Scorecard is that the debts related to college can be measured in terms of monetary obligations between individual students and the federal government. In a private transaction, students are buying a product from a university, and when the monetary debt is paid off, one might imagine that the obligations would disappear. But we would argue that the debts and obligations related to attending college are much more complex and actually help bind individuals together in a democratic society. Everyone involved with higher education must consider these mutual obligations more carefully—as hard as that can be when so many of us are weighed down by debt.

6

Average Wages
by College Major

In 2015, Georgetown University's Center on Education and the Work-force published a major report that estimated "the economic benefit of earning an advanced degree by undergraduate major."[1] Analyzing responses to the Census Bureau's massive American Community Survey, the report found that employed college graduates who majored in engineering—especially metallurgical and mining engineering—had average annual earnings that were more than double the average wages earned by graduates with lower-paying majors such as early childhood and elementary education. This wage disparity seemed to persist throughout employees' careers. The authors calculate that "the top-paying college majors earn $3.4 million more than the lowest-paying majors over a lifetime."[2] That difference is even larger than the gap between the average earnings of people with and without bachelor's degrees.

These statistics suggest that the major you choose could have a greater impact on your future earnings than the decision to go to college. But are statistics on average wages by major, which are now pervasive in the United States, actually a good source of information as you're making a decision about which college major(s) to pursue? Unfortunately, as with the metrics discussed in the previous chapters, wage-by-major statistics are filled with hidden assumptions and can be difficult to interpret accurately. This chapter will explain what these

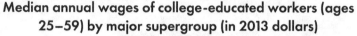

FIGURE 6.1.

Median annual wages of college-educated workers (ages 25–59) by major supergroup (in 2013 dollars)

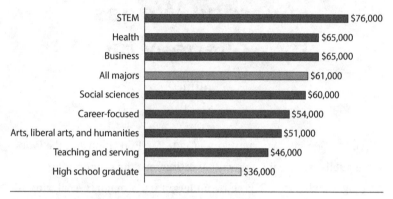

STEM	$76,000
Health	$65,000
Business	$65,000
All majors	$61,000
Social sciences	$60,000
Career-focused	$54,000
Arts, liberal arts, and humanities	$51,000
Teaching and serving	$46,000
High school graduate	$36,000

Source: Anthony P. Carnevale and Jeff Strohl, *Separate & Unequal* (Washington, DC: Georgetown University Center on Education and the Workforce, 2013), https://1gyhoq 479ufd3yna29x7ubjn-wpengine.netdna-ssl.com/wp-content/uploads/SeparateUnequal.ES_.pdf.

statistics are trying to accomplish, how the economists that produce them come to their conclusions, what some of the common flaws are, and why you should be very cautious when you use them to make the important decision of what to study in college.

Let's begin by returning to the Georgetown study from the first paragraph. Figure 6.1 summarizes the report's main findings. It shows that full-time mid-career employees with bachelor's degrees in science, technology, engineering, and mathematics (STEM) fields had an average income of $76,000 per year in the early 2010s, more than double the average income of high school graduates who did not attend college. This is also far higher than the average income of college graduates as a whole, which was $61,000. While college graduates with majors in business or health-oriented fields such as pharmacy and nursing also earned above-average wages, those with "career-focused" professional majors such as agriculture and communications and students with degrees in the arts and humanities earned below-average wages. Graduates with majors in teaching and serving fields (which include psychology and social work) earned the lowest average salaries. Their average annual wage was $46,000, 40% lower than the average wages of STEM majors.

What are we meant to do with this information? One motivation for publishing the average wages employees earn according to their field of study is to convince current university students to choose majors that the statistics suggest will lead them to high-earning careers. In 2016, the *New York Times* noted that economist Andrew Carnevale, the main author of the Georgetown report, "argues that there should be much more information available to students about employment and wage prospects before they choose a major so that they can make informed choices. 'We don't want to take away Shakespeare. We're just talking about helping people make good decisions.'"[3] Put differently, the idea behind this metric is that colleges should be as transparent as possible about what sort of financial future you can expect when you are choosing a major.

Many politicians and university administrators agree. The agencies that manage the major public university systems of California and Texas have built interactive websites that allow prospective and current students to see average wages by major for each of their campuses.[4] The American Institutes for Research created a new research group, College Matters, to produce wage-by-major reports and online tools for universities. Colorado, Minnesota, Tennessee, and Virginia were among the states that hired College Matters to estimate and publicize wage-by-major statistics for their public university systems.[5] The Democratic commissioner of the Minnesota Office of Higher Education explained: "As the cost of higher education increases, so does the pressure on students to choose a major that will lead to a good-paying job. This website offers data-based trends specific to Minnesota that can help students and families make informed decisions."[6] In a testament to the political potency of College Matters, the organization's president left his position in early 2018 to join the Trump administration as director of the U.S. Department of Education's Institute of Education Sciences.[7]

The fact that a broad political coalition supports the dissemination of wage-by-major statistics could suggest that they provide invaluable and uncontroversial information to students. But do students and families pay attention to these statistics when making decisions? Let's take a look at how students tend to use them.

Do Students Care about Future Wages?

In 2010, economists Matthew Wiswall and Basit Zafar set out to study the impact of average-wage-by-major statistics on student choices. They were interested in how students' beliefs changed when they were presented with wage-by-major statistics like those currently being rolled out across the United States. They started with a simple question: Do students care about average wage statistics when they're choosing what to study in college?

Wiswall and Zafar paid 500 undergraduate students at New York University to complete a detailed survey. They collected information about students' beliefs about average postgraduate wages by major and the students' expectations about what their postgraduate wages would be if they pursued a variety of majors. Afterward, Wiswall and Zafar showed students actual average wage statistics for male and female employees in four categories of majors: business, engineering, humanities, and natural sciences. They also showed them the average wages of students who did not graduate. Then they asked the students again about their expectations about future wages.

Do students care about their own future expected earnings in different majors when they're choosing a field of study? The answer, Wiswall and Zafar found, is a resounding yes.[8] But some of the other results of this study are also very interesting.

First, NYU students weren't very good at estimating average postgraduate wages by major. On average, they were off by about 40%—a gap of tens of thousands of dollars in most cases. Students' errors also followed a consistent pattern; on average, the students overestimated postgraduate wages for business and humanities majors and underestimated wages for engineering majors.

After the students were given objective information about average wages by major in the United States, they were asked again about the wages that they would expect to earn (*themselves*, not on average) if they ended up earning each of several different majors. Some students changed their estimates after they saw accurate population-level information about average wages by major, and those students said that they would be more likely to choose majors that they thought would lead them to higher earnings. Students who participated in the experiment reported that they were an average of 4 percentage points less likely to pursue a degree in the humanities and an average of 2.5 percentage points more likely to pursue degrees in engineering and computer science.

Interestingly, the researchers found that students were surprisingly resistant to using average-wage-by-major statistics—which reported national averages across all working ages—to update their beliefs about their own future incomes. Let's take a male first-year student who plans on being a business major and expects to earn $80,000 a few years after graduating. This student thinks that engineering majors earn about $66,000 on average but also thinks that if he switched his major to engineering, he would be able to beat that average and make $75,000. Then he's given the news: actually, male engineering majors earned an average of $82,000, about 20% more than his original $66,000 estimate. When the student has this new information, by how much does he revise his original guess about how much he would earn with a degree in engineering?

It turns out that his revision is small: on average, he would increase his estimate by just 1.6%, to $76,200. Despite his fairly large underestimation of engineering majors' average wages, having access to accurate information would only make him about 4% more likely to switch to engineering. The bottom line is that students appear to treat this information with caution. As we will discuss in detail in the next section, this turns out to be a good idea.

Wiswall and Zafar ran their experiment a few years before organizations across the country began to popularize wage-by-major information. But since 2010, significant improvements in data visualization, data quality, and data specificity have likely increased the degree to which students pay attention to wage-by-major statistics and use them as a basis for deciding which major to pursue in college.

Figure 6.2 shows the online Alumni at Work tool that the University of California built to display the average wages of its alumni. For any campus, graduation year, and major, students can see the 25th, 50th, and 75th percentiles of wages of alumni in that group two, five, and ten years after graduation. Students can compare those wages across campuses and majors. Additional tabs show the distribution of industries in which UC alumni work and a student debt calculator that shows the average amount of time it takes alumni to pay back their loans. With tools like Alumni at Work providing somewhat personalized statistics about expected wages, students can use these statistics to form beliefs about what they can expect to earn across fields of study. Wiswall and Zafar's study implies that these adjustments will contribute to students' choice of college major.

Interpreting Wage-by-Major Statistics

It is a maxim among most economists that, as Wiswall and Zafar put it, "providing students with accurate information can only be welfare enhancing."[9] This belief is widely shared across the political spectrum.

But wage-by-major statistics are deceivingly tricky for first-year students to interpret. Take, for example, the fact that anthropology majors earn lower median wages than history majors by about 10% (or

FIGURE 6.2.

The University of California Alumni at Work dashboard

University of California
Alumni at Work
LIVING AND WORKING IN CALIFORNIA

The majority (~74%) of UC Alumni live and work in California. Information in this dashboard shows typical annual earnings of UC undergraduate alumni who work in California, by campus, discipline, major and whether or not they went on to complete a graduate degree (at UC or another institution). While information on alumni working outside of California is not yet available, data from this dashboard is the most comprehensive resource available to understand earning potential of UC undergraduate alumni.

Undergraduate UC Campus	Graduation Year	Undergraduate Discipline	Major	Completed Graduate Degree
(All) ▼	(All) ▼	(All) ▼	(All) ▼	(All) ▼

Typical Annual Earnings: All
Campus: All   Discipline: All
Major: All

The chart below shows the middle range of UC alumni earnings salaries for the selected major or discipline using the 25th percentile, median and 75th percentile. The range in salary shows a likely range of salaries for alumni with this major at 2, 5 and 10 years after graduation.

UC Comparisons of Annual Earnings

The chart below shows the typical annual earnings for the major selected compared to all UC graduates and compared to students who attended other four year colleges in California. Note: The Graduation Year filter does not apply to this chart.

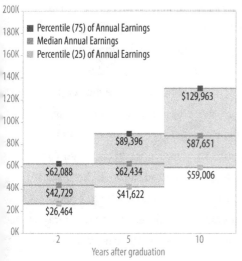

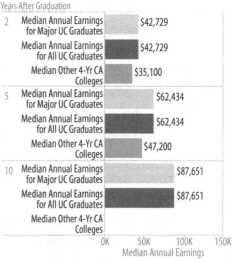

Note: 25% of graduates earn salaries greater than the top of the blue range and 25% earn salaries below the bottom of the blue range. Information is supressed for data points with less than 30 alumni.

Note: Data from "Other four year colleges" is from the USDOE College Scorecard, which includes students enrolled 6-year and 10 years ago. Includes students who may or may not have graduated. This data is for recipients of Title IV financial aid only and is not diferentiated by major.

Note: UC's dashboard shows median wages by major and number of years after graduation, but only for UC graduates working in California.

Source: University of California, "University Alumni at Work," accessed May 23, 2022, https://www.universityofcalifornia.edu/about-us/information-center/uc-alumni-work.

$5,000 each year) according to the Georgetown report discussed at the beginning of the chapter. One reason for this difference may be that an education in history increases a student's labor market value—perhaps through the development of critical reading and writing skills or because reading history texts cultivates a transferable attention to detail—that enables them to earn higher wages when they seek employment after graduation. According to this explanation, if a student intending to major in anthropology decided to switch and major in history instead, she could expect to increase her future earnings by around 10%. That might be enough of a difference to motivate some students to switch from one major to the other.

But there are many alternative explanations for these differences in postgraduate wages, each of which we'll discuss in more detail below. Maybe the kind of students who would earn a high wage *no matter what college major they choose* are more likely to prefer history to anthropology, which makes history look more lucrative than anthropology even though a history degree doesn't provide any additional educational value. Maybe universities push high-achieving students into certain majors, making those fields look more lucrative. Maybe people who chose some majors are more likely to be omitted from the employment data used to produce wage estimates. People could be omitted for a number of reasons: because they are more likely to go to graduate school instead of getting a job after graduation or because they are more likely to drop out of college or not find a job after graduation. Maybe the wages of current employees in the underlying data are a poor proxy for the wages today's students will earn twenty or thirty years down the line.

Each of these explanations challenges the inference from wage-by-major statistics that if you switched from a lower-earning major to a higher-earning major, your future earnings would increase. This is hugely important, because remember that the key purpose of these statistics is to help you decide whether to choose a major that will lead to higher wages than your preferred major will. Below, we'll tackle each of those concerns, some of which pose a bigger challenge than others. The problems come in three varieties. *Selection* problems refer to differences in the kinds of students who choose each major. *Measurement* problems relate to the nuts and bolts of how wage-by-major averages are calculated. *Extrapolation* problems relate to whether the available statistics are relevant to any specific student who is choosing a major right now.

Selection Problems with Average-Wage-by-Major Statistics
Selection Problem I: Entry Requirements

Many universities limit which students are permitted to choose certain fields of study. Some of these limits are implemented as early as when a student applies to attend their institution. For example, many universities require high school students to directly apply to engineering programs if they want to earn an engineering major, which often requires higher standardized test scores or good grades in specific high school science courses. Other limits are imposed after students have completed one or more semesters of college. First-year students may have to earn certain grades in introductory courses before they are allowed to major in nursing or economics; sophomores might have to apply to a university's business administration major, perhaps on the basis of their leadership activities during their first year of college. Universities may also impose soft requirements intended to push students out of certain majors. For example, professors may try to discourage students from majoring in chemistry by giving lower average grades or by giving preference to students who completed advanced high school courses when admitting students to the department's introductory course.

Consider, for example, a university where students are required to earn a B+ average in four introductory courses before declaring a major in computer science. A number of student characteristics could explain why a given student—let's call her Jessica, as in Chapter 2—is able to successfully meet this requirement while some of her peers cannot. Jessica might be an above-average math student, which would help her get good grades in difficult introductory courses. She might have substantial self-motivation to work hard in the course or be unusually willing to spend long hours studying. Either of these things would likely give her a comparative advantage on exams. If she doesn't have to work at a job or satisfy family responsibilities during college, she may have more time to dedicate to the course than her peers. If she attended a high school that offered advanced computer science courses, she might already know a great deal of the material taught in the introductory courses. Finally, if she can afford a private tutor, she has an advantage over students who don't have the resources for that kind of help.

No matter which of these reasons explains how Jessica is able to satisfy the requirements and major in computer science, that same reason might also explain how she may end up earning a high wage after graduation, regardless of whether or not she pursued the computer science major. Employees with above-average mathematical capabilities or high self-motivation will likely earn high wages no matter which college major they choose. People who received a high-quality high school education or who don't have to work while in college or who can afford a tutor are often from high-income families, which in turn provide socialization and networks that can help them find high-wage employment. If the computer science department at this university admitted everyone to its major, its average postgraduate wages would likely be much lower because the earnings of its stellar graduates would have to be averaged in with the earnings of graduates who had less motivation or who came from less-advantaged backgrounds. But this change in the composition of students in the computer science major would not necessarily mean that the value of the major for any particular student had decreased.

While not all universities restrict entry to specific majors, the majors most likely to be restricted at any university are those with high average postgraduate wages. Departments in the STEM fields in particular are known to discourage students from pursuing their majors. As early as the 1970s, a nationally representative survey of third-year college students showed that 42% of students who entered college intending to study the natural sciences had switched out of those disciplines, compared to just 23–24% of students in all other disciplines.[10] The survey results suggest that as many as 15–20% of students who intended to major in the sciences had been pushed out.[11]

Interestingly, despite the increased likelihood that students who initially intend to major in a STEM discipline will be pushed into a different field of study, those students are not more likely to drop out of college completely.[12] However, since university major requirements tend to admit students with strong labor market prospects into STEM majors—due to the strong positive correlation between academic opportunities before attending college, academic preparation, and family income—the students who are pushed out are likely to have somewhat poorer prospects. Their postgraduate earnings may lower the average wage statistics of less restrictive majors in the humanities and social sciences.

The net effect of the various policies that restrict access to certain majors is to make the positive wage effects of those majors look larger than the actual causal effect of choosing to earn that major. Without a centralized database of the nationwide prevalence and stringency of university policies for restricting access to majors, it is difficult to estimate how much they contribute to the high average wages among graduates who majored in computer science, economics, engineering, and other frequently restricted majors. However, the selection effect may be substantial.

Selection Problem II:
Student Employment Preferences

Let's go back to Jessica, our hypothetical student who is more likely to choose a high-earning major than many of her peers. The last section discussed the possibility that Jessica's university might implicitly encourage her to choose a high-earning major. But Jessica might not need that encouragement; she might be someone who already has a strong preference for a high-earning job (compared to the earnings from a stable job or a job where you never have to work evenings or a job that provides personal fulfillment). If Jessica believes that certain majors are more likely to lead her to a high-paying job—perhaps because she thinks that the major's curriculum will prepare her to work in a high-wage industry, or maybe because she's seen statistics showing that students who have completed those majors have higher average post-graduate earnings—she might choose those majors on her own, without any encouragement. This could cause a positive feedback loop in which high-earning majors becoming *even more* high earning because they attract wage-driven students.

In a follow-up to their study discussed above, Wiswall and Zafar asked their cohort of NYU students how they thought about the benefits and costs of certain jobs.[13] For example, they asked which fields students believed would lead them to high-paying jobs, to jobs where employees were rarely fired, or to jobs with greater time flexibility for hours worked. They also asked which factors mattered to these students. The survey results showed a lot of variation between students. Some students wanted high-paying jobs, but others (especially women) placed far greater value on flexibility and a low probability of being fired.

Wiswall and Zafar followed up with their sample of students a few years after they had graduated. They found that the preferences study participants articulated while they were still students were highly correlated with the jobs they had. Participants who wanted higher wages when they were in college ended up in jobs with higher wages. More interestingly, they found that students' relative preferences about wages, flexibility, and stability were important to their choice of major. Most students told the researchers that they believed that business majors would lead them to higher-paying jobs (in finance, for example) and that majors in the humanities would lead people to jobs with greater flexibility and stability (in education or public administration, for example). As a result, students sorted themselves across majors in accordance with their beliefs. Those who wanted high wages majored in business and generally ended up with high-wage jobs, while those who wanted flexibility majored in the humanities and mostly got the flexibility they desired.

This brings us back to the key selection problem at the center of wage-by-major statistics. Regardless of what students believed and what their academic and sociodemographic qualities were before they came to college, did majoring in business increase their earnings after college? We know that business majors have higher average wages than humanities majors, but is this *because* the students studied business or is it because the kind of student who wants high wages will choose to study business even if that student would still have been able to obtain a high-earning job if they had majored in the humanities? To look at it another way: let's assume that Jessica doesn't want to work as a manager in a large firm. For her, then, studying business might not increase her future wages. After all, the primary reason business majors earn so much money might be that they studied business because they wanted to be corporate managers (and earn corporate managers' salaries), not because having a business degree substantially increased their employability as managers at large firms. You certainly don't have to be a business major to be a corporate manager; as of 2019, only 30% of college-educated U.S. managers had business degrees, while 13% had degrees in the arts and humanities.[14] Do business majors have high earnings because of what they learned or because their choice of major reflects their preexisting preferences?

Wiswall and Zafar don't estimate the degree to which student employment preferences distort wage-by-major statistics, but this is a second reason to be cautious about making predictions about a given student's wage (or how their wages could change in different scenarios) using average wage-by-major statistics.

Selection Problem III: The Measured Academic Aptitude of Students

According to a recent report by *Business Insider*, economics is the most popular major at six of the seven private Ivy League universities (only finance is more popular at the seventh Ivy League school, the University of Pennsylvania). Until recently, political science or government were the next most popular majors at five of those seven schools.[15] But outside the Ivy League, neither economics nor political science is anywhere close to the most popular undergraduate major. The Georgetown wage report we started the chapter with shows that among all college-educated employees in the United States, economics and political science are ranked 15th and 16th, respectively, trailing behind professional degrees such as business and nursing and liberal arts degrees in fields such as English, psychology, and biology.[16]

The report also shows that economics and political science are the social science majors with the highest average postgraduate wages. The average earnings of economics majors are 50% higher than the earnings of employees who majored in sociology or anthropology. One factor contributing to these high wages is the high measured academic aptitude of the students who choose those majors, since those students disproportionately attend Ivy League and other elite universities. These majors likely generate particularly high returns for top students. Harvard students, for example, are substantially overrepresented in the senior financial and governmental positions that economics and political science degrees from Harvard would prepare them for. But that doesn't necessarily mean that switching into those majors at other universities will raise the wages students can expect.

This "academic sorting"—the way that students of different measurable academic aptitude and preparation (as measured by high school grades or exams such as the SAT) tend to choose different majors—presents an additional challenge for how to use wage-by-major statistics. One key dimension of academic sorting that economist Peter Arcidiacono identified in his detailed study of the subject is math capability.[17] If Jessica is a strong math student, then she is likely to attend a higher-quality university and may have a preference for studying majors that let her use her mathematical capabilities. Is Jessica's high postgraduate wage the result of the high-quality university she attended, the math-heavy major she earned, or the mathematical prowess that helped her obtain her university degree? The average-wage-by-major statistics and interactive data visualizations that universities publish on their websites do not disentangle those factors.

Arcidiacono estimates that in the 1980s, 32-year-olds who majored in a STEM field earned about 39% more than students who did not have a college degree but that about half of the wage difference could be explained by all three of the selection problems we have described in this section. His findings are similar for other college majors. This suggests that a meaningful portion of the average difference in wages between any two majors can be explained by which kinds of students happen to earn degrees in those fields, not the relative impact that earning a degree in one of those fields would likely have on a student. Arcidiacono's findings give a sense of the role that students' nonrandom selection of college majors plays in driving differences in average wages by major and thus gives us another reason to question the usefulness of these statistics as you choose between fields of study.

Measurement Problems with Wage-by-Major Statistics

Measurement Problem I: Low-Quality Data

We will now leave selection problems behind and move on to discuss some of the problems related to how these statistics are calculated. The first chapter of this book discussed the limitations of the wage statistics PayScale publishes. PayScale's wage data are self-reported by a self-selected sample of U.S. employees. The data may be modified in unknown ways prior to statistical estimation. The sample size of the data in each category—the number of people who attended a given school, majored in a given field, and reported their earnings to PayScale—is often small, which leads to dubious estimates of average wages. While each of these problems is specific to PayScale, each also represents the many ways that low-quality data decreases the usefulness of wage-by-major statistics.

Consider, for example, the UC Alumni at Work dashboard (from fig. 6.2 a few pages ago) that provides wage-by-major statistics for graduates from University of California campuses.[18] First, the available data only include employees living in the state of California who are not self-employed and do not work for the federal government. This includes only about 50% of UC graduates ten years after graduation; the large numbers of financially successful small business owners or alumni who have emigrated out of the state are excluded. Second, the data are "annualized" before they are averaged, which means that UC inflates graduates' observed wages when earnings are not reported in all four quarters of a given year. This process may relatively benefit the average wages for some majors. For example, many jobs in the arts do not pay wages during the summer but the university extrapolates wages from other months to "fill in" missing quarters in the data, resulting in wage-by-major statistics in the arts that are artificially high relative to other fields.[19] Finally, the dashboard website does not provide data about sample sizes. However, the fact that the dashboard has no data from alumni in many of the majors listed on the website (in fact, clicking on them causes the online interactive chart to disappear) suggests that small samples may skew the estimates.

Some wage-by-major estimates are better than others. The Georgetown estimates, for example, are generated from a survey database that does not exclude any employees and is large enough to remove the statistical uncertainty that could accompany smaller data sets like PayScale's. However, it cannot provide averages for any specific university since the survey respondents are not asked about which school they attended. Although the federal College Scorecard uses IRS tax records to provide well-measured wage-by-major statistics by university, even those data are imperfect because they exclude the many alumni who did not receive federal financial aid when they were enrolled as students. While different available data sources have different benefits and costs, none wholly avoid measurement challenges, and just a small number of measurement issues can compound to substantially bias available statistics when taken together.

Measurement Problem II: Missing Data

A number of fundamental limitations are baked into the calculation of all wage-by-major statistics that make them less useful to students who are choosing a major. First, most of the data used to construct wage-by-major statistics includes only individuals who have graduated from college. If students who declare certain majors and attempt to complete them have a higher likelihood of dropping out of college, then the effect of choosing those majors may not be clear from statistics that include only people who have completed the major. For example, in their in-depth study of students at Berea College, a small no-tuition liberal arts college in Kentucky, economists Ralph and Todd Stinebrickner showed that students who enroll at Berea intending to study professional fields such as education and agriculture are more likely to drop out of college than students who major in other fields.[20] As a result, first-year students looking at the average wages of Berea graduates should keep in mind that the average wages for agriculture alumni are likely even lower than wage-by-major statistics would suggest, since the statistics omit many former agriculture majors who dropped out and are now likely earning lower mid-career wages than their peers who graduated. Estimating wages by the major former students *selected* (including those who quit) rather than the major that group *completed* could produce more accurate income data. We'll return to this idea a bit later.

Second, income data usually only include the reported incomes of people who are currently employed. This excludes unemployed people, homemakers, and employees who earn unreported "off-the-book" wages. As a result, majors such as primary education that lead graduates to low-paying jobs will have artificially low wage-by-major averages relative to a major such as linguistics that tends to lead graduates to unemployment (the major with the highest unemployment rate in 2017 for people aged 40), since the unemployed linguistics students (and students in other fields with high unemployment) are excluded from the estimating sample.[21]

Finally, because of cost-of-living differences in different geographic regions, wage data may not correspond to college graduates' quality of life. Psychology is the most popular major among employees in about half of US states. Most of the ten states with the highest proportion of psychology majors in their workforce are in the Northeast, a region with relatively high prices for food, housing, and energy. Most of the ten states with the highest proportion of biology majors in their workforce, on the other hand, are in the Southeast, where prices are much lower. Some proportion of these price differences can likely be explained by differences in the quality of available goods and services (for example, in return for higher prices, residents of the Northeast may get higher-quality local amenities or better living arrangements), but the rest reflects a real difference in cost of living in the two regions.[22] As a result, graduates with biology degrees (who tend to live in the Southeast) may be better off compared to graduates with psychology degrees (who tend to live in the Northeast) than wage-by-major statistics suggest, since the biology degree holders tend to work in places where they can buy more for each dollar than a typical psychology degree holder can.[23]

These issues may look negligible, but like problems with data quality, they can add up to substantial biases in wage-by-major statistics. None of these problems would be fixed by improving the sample size or the coverage of the data that is the basis for the current wage-by-major statistics. Instead, it would be necessary for statisticians to collect additional data points (for example, the intended majors of people who dropped out of college), make imputations (of unreported wages, for example), and make adjustments (correcting for cost-of-living differences, for example) in order to produce more helpful statistics for young college students.

Extrapolation Problems with Wage-by-Major Statistics
Extrapolation Problem I: Short-Run Wages, Short-Term Thinking

The curricula at universities change over time, and you might think that it's important to collect wage-by-major data from recent graduates to get a strong sense of the employment outcomes that would be relevant for current students. That seems to have been the thinking of the Minnesota Office of Higher Education, which recently produced an interactive wage-by-major dashboard. The dashboard showed separate average earnings statistics for each Minnesota institution and each major for all students who had graduated two or four years earlier.[24]

Minnesota's dashboard showed some surprising trends. For example, construction management was in the top twelve most lucrative majors at the University of Minnesota Twin Cities two years after graduation,

while neurobiology and biochemistry were among the twelve least lucrative majors. Employed students with construction management degrees earn almost four times the average wage of neurobiology majors
two years after graduation.

How should these statistics be interpreted? One explanation is that
construction management has led students to a higher-paying career
trajectory than biochemistry. But a more likely explanation is that many
biochemistry majors attend graduate school after completing their undergraduate degree, and while they are in graduate school, they earn
low wages as they prepare for more lucrative future careers. Indeed,
the Georgetown report shows that more than two-thirds of biochemistry and neuroscience majors in the national workforce have earned
graduate degrees and that biochemistry majors have average mid-
career earnings of $97,000, far higher than the average wages of
graduates with degrees in the category that includes construction management. The bottom line is that wages estimated two or four years
after graduation are likely to be biased by graduate school attendance,
early career employment changes, and all of the frictions that delay
young peoples' entry into the labor market.

In part as an attempt to overcome the flaws of these short time
frames, economist Raj Chetty and his colleagues studied income patterns for graduates across universities for fourteen years after graduation using detailed IRS tax records.[25] They found that as late as age
26, when many students are four years out of college, the income of
graduates of elite Ivy League universities was indistinguishable from
that of graduates from any other four-year university. The income of
these two groups of graduates diverges when they are 27 to 32 years
old, such that 32-year-old Ivy League graduates earned far more than
graduates of other universities at the same age. Chetty and his colleagues argued that wage comparisons across universities stabilize when
graduates are ages 32 to 36 and that estimating wages at earlier ages
can lead to large miscalculations.

The best available evidence suggests that by the time graduates are in their early 30s, the wage-by-major ranking has roughly stabilized. In ongoing research at the University of California, Zachary Bleemer has shown that computer science is the highest-earning major at UC Berkeley ten years after graduation. Graduates who majored in that field earn about twice the average wage of humanities majors. This finding is stable even when the data reaches back decades. The highest-earning major thirty years after people graduated from UC Berkeley in the early 1970s was computer science. The median earnings of that group in the early 2000s was just about double the average wage of people who majored in the humanities. How about forty years after graduation, this time for people who graduated in the late 1960s? It's computer science again; the median earnings of that group in the late 2000s was almost double the average wage of humanities majors. The rankings look similar all the way down; people who took degrees in business and economics earn high incomes, people who took degrees in humanities fields and vocational disciplines earn low incomes, and people who took degrees in the social and natural sciences have earnings that are in between.[26]

While wage-by-major statistics using wage data for people aged 32 are highly correlated with similar statistics estimated at older ages, they still have many limitations, as we've shown above. These limitations are compounded for statistics that use income data for employees who are younger than 32. Estimates of income from data collected from people who are just a few years after college can grossly mislead first-year students who are seeking majors that will lead them toward remunerative employment.

Extrapolation Problem II: Match Quality and Preferences

Wage-by-major statistics could also not be relevant to current students because any specific student has a lot of differences from the "average" student that wage-by-major statistics describe. After all, which major will lead a *specific* student to high postgraduate wages might depend a lot on characteristics of that student, like their mathematical or writing capabilities, their preferences for certain subject matter, their study habits, or even their dreams about what they want for themselves in the future. How much can any student learn from data drawn from median statistics about employees who chose a specific college major?

This question brings us to a recent academic study that overcame many of the challenges described above. The study estimates differences in wages across fields that are adjusted for all of the selection concerns noted above. It compares near-identical students who are almost randomly assigned to different majors and compares their wages years after graduation. The wage data are high quality and cover every employee in the entire country. The study even includes students who had selected a major but then dropped out of college. And it focuses on students who are torn between two fields, showing what would happen if they were to select one or the other. This is a group of students whose outcomes are likely of great interest to first-year college students who are trying to decide between two majors.

The study also has some limitations. It focuses on wages at age 30 or before, which may not accurately reflect differences in wages across peoples' careers. Also, the study analyzes students who attended college in Norway, not the United States, and Norway's universities and labor markets are somewhat different from those in the United States. Nevertheless, the statistics estimated by economists Lars Kirkeboen, Edwin Leuven, and Magne Mogstad offer important insight into the usefulness of wage-by-major statistics and into which majors students choose.[27]

In order to explain what the economists learned, it's going to be important for you to understand how college admissions works in Norway. Unlike the United States, Norway has one centralized office that administers admissions for every university in Norway. Students submit a ranked list of university-major pairs that they would like to attend. For example, they might list economics at the University of Oslo first, economics at the University of Bergen second, philosophy at the University of Oslo third, and so on. Students are allowed to list up to fifteen rank-ordered university-major preferences on their application.

A computer algorithm determines which students are admitted to which programs. Human beings do not make any decisions about which student gets admitted to which department at which university. Each student is assigned an "application score," which is mostly determined by their high school grades. Students with the highest score are admitted to their first-choice school and major. Then students with the second-best score are admitted. As the algorithm goes down the list, eventually some of the more popular university-major pairs fill up. Unassigned students who listed those programs as their first choice are then assigned to their second-choice program. The algorithm continues down the list of scores and places students into programs and universities that were lower and lower on their list of preferences as all of their preferred programs fill up. Once all of the program slots have been filled or all of the students have been assigned, the admissions process is complete and students are notified of the field they will be studying and the school they will be attending the following year.

Kirkeboen, Leuven, and Mogstad decided to compare the postgraduate wages of students who *just barely* made it into their preferred program, the ones who were assigned to the last available slots before the program filled up, with the postgraduate wages of students who just barely missed making it into the program they preferred and were assigned to their next-most-preferred program instead. These students likely only differed from each other by one or two points on their application score: it's as if one of them got an A- in their sophomore year history course and the other got a B+ in that course and for that reason alone, the former student got into their preferred university department and the latter got their next-best choice instead. You can

TABLE 6.1.

Estimated wage value of completing a degree in a discipline (rows) for people who would have otherwise enrolled in their next-best alternative discipline (columns), in thousands of dollars

| | NEXT-BEST ALTERNATIVE | | | |
COMPLETED DEGREE	HUMANITIES	SOCIAL SCIENCES	SCIENCES	ENGINEERING
Humanities	—	21.4*	5.0	–38.5**
Social sciences	18.7**	—	55.5**	–55.4**
Sciences	53.7**	69.6**	—	–2.2
Engineering	59.8	–5.5	52.4**	—

Source: Data from estimates for earnings of college graduates in their late 20s in Norway in Lars J. Kirkeboen, Edwin Leuven, and Magne Mogstad, "Field of Study, Earnings, and Self-Selection," *Quarterly Journal of Economics* 131, no. 3 (2016): 1057–1111.

Note: The table shows the estimated change in thousands of dollars of earnings eight years after applying to college if a person had completed a degree in the "completed degree" field compared to their earnings if they hadn't had access to that field and were admitted to their less-preferred "next-best alternative" field instead. Asterisks indicate statistical significance from 0 at the 10% (*) and 5% (**) levels.

probably see why comparing the subsequent lives of these on-the-margin students is particularly interesting: given the small score differences between them, it's almost as if access to the more-preferred department was based on something like the flip of a coin and only one of the students got in. The two students hardly differed from each other before going to college, but now they're enrolling in different college majors. If they end up with different postgraduate wages in later years, it's probably because they studied different things, not for any of the other reasons that we've discussed in the previous sections (like different student preferences or differential university access).

You can see a subset of the scholars' findings in Table 6.1. It presents information Kirkeboen, Leuven, and Mogstad collected about Norwegian workers eight years after they applied to attend college, or about four years after they graduated. The units are in thousands of dollars in annual earnings. You can read the table by choosing two disciplines: the discipline in which a student actually earned their college degree (along the left-hand side) and that student's next-best alternative if they hadn't gotten into that program. The table reports the average additional wages earned by people who were able to complete a degree in each field separately by the disciplines that they would have studied if they hadn't gotten into that field. The asterisks tell us how confident Kirkeboen, Leuven, and Mogstad are that the numbers in the table reflect the effect of earning degrees in students' more-preferred fields as opposed to reflecting random chance, with more asterisks indicating greater confidence.

Let's take a look at an example. Look at the top left-hand number in the table. This number is essentially produced by comparing the wages of two groups of Norwegian students. Both groups of students would have preferred to study a social science field to studying a humanities field and both were very close to being admitted to the social science field. But some of them had scores that were *just* high enough for them to be admitted to study social science and others had scores that were *just* too low, which meant that they studied a humanities field instead. A comparison between these two groups' wages several years later shows that the people who earned social science degrees were earning about $18,700 more than the people who were admitted to humanities degrees instead. That's a big effect, suggesting that studying social science is a lucrative choice for people who prefer social science to the humanities.

But now take a look at the number just above and to the right of that one. Now the situation is reversed: we're looking at students with a preference for studying humanities but some of them had slightly lower scores and had to study social science as their next-best alternative instead. There's something surprising here: the reported number, $21,400, is also positive! This means that the people in this group who earned humanities degrees were earning more than those who were admitted to social science instead. That's also a big effect, and in the opposite direction: studying humanities is a lucrative choice for people who prefer humanities to social science.

In fact, if you look at the first three columns and first three rows of Table 6.1, you'll see that all six numbers are greater than zero. In other words, the value of earning a college degree in the liberal arts and sciences seems to depend a lot on students' preferences. Earning a degree in the field that the students *want* to earn a degree in—as reflected in the rank-ordered preferences that students submit when they apply to Norwegian universities—tends to increase their early-career earnings, even if that field is in a relatively lower-paying field like the humanities. Conversely, being pushed into a field that the students would prefer *not* to study tends to decrease their early-career earnings, even if that field is in a relatively higher-paying field like the sciences.

It appears that the wages of humanities, social science, and science majors importantly depend on students' preferences. *Whichever field the student prefers, completing that major will lead them to higher wages.* Kirkeboen, Leuven, and Mogstad refer to this as "comparative advantage": students' preferences align with their strengths, and following their preferences can improve their future earnings.

Of course, comparative advantage only goes so far. The last column of Table 6.1 shows that in terms of their average future wages, students who considered engineering as a potential major would have been better off majoring in engineering, whether or not they prefer humanities or social science. Nevertheless, these statistics simultaneously call into question the purpose of average wage-by-major statistics and point toward a potential (and far more useful) replacement. Studying students who are on the fence between two majors and measuring postgraduate wages for people who made one or another choice for different reasons (looking at, say, the average wages of students whose parents pushed them to major in STEM compared to those who felt less pressure and thus majored in something else) could provide an effective alternative to the current wage-by-major statistics that are available in the United States, although unfortunately such statistics are currently available only in rare circumstances.[28]

Can Wage-by-Major Statistics Be Salvaged?

Future wages are one of many factors relevant to a college student's choice of major. Imagine the ideal tool that a student would want when considering the effect of their college major on their future wages. They would want to provide information about themselves: their capabilities, their preferences, their goals, where they saw themselves in eight or ten years in their private lives (i.e., whether or not they would be caring for young children). Then they would want to see what has happened to people like them who made a variety of choices. If a strong math student is choosing between majoring in English and chemistry, for example, then she might want to know the average career paths and wages of other strong math students who had made one or the other choice.

The student might derive a small amount of insight from Kirkeboen, Leuven, and Mogstad's study, from which she would learn that Norwegian students who chose to major in English over chemistry earned similar wages to those who majored in science instead. While imperfect, that information could help inform the student's decision. "Know thy preferences" is a key takeaway from this chapter. No matter what your long-term objectives are, preferences importantly shape the impacts of major on student outcomes and should be an important determinant of which major you choose.

The wage-by-major statistics that are currently available in the United States, however, would be substantially less helpful. While English majors earn less than chemistry majors on average, the discrepancy can be explained in a lot of ways, including preexisting differences in which students earn each major (and at which schools they earn them), data anomalies, and mismeasurement. Even in the absence of those discrepancies, extrapolating from those statistics to estimate what an individual student might earn would be challenging because studying certain fields might have different effects on people's labor market outcomes in different decades and different effects for students with different interests and employment preferences. With these factors in mind, it is unclear how students should integrate the relevant wage-by-major statistics into their decision, let alone choose one major over another on the basis of these statistics.

Of course, the fact that many current and future wage-by-major statistics are largely unhelpful to—and easily mislead—current college students is not in itself a reason to throw those statistics away. On the one hand, the presentation of such estimates contributes to the rhetoric that sees people as "human capital," implicitly teaching students to value future employment and wages above other considerations. That mindset may lead students to make unwise decisions about which major to choose. On the other hand, Wiswall and Zafar have shown that the likely net result of making students aware of wage-by-major statistics is to make them more likely to earn science and engineering degrees.[29] While it's not clear that this choice is optimal for all students, it may benefit society if the students end up innovating and/or designing public goods and it aligns with a series of reports from the National Academies of Science, Engineering, and Medicine that have advocated for increasing the number of students who earn STEM majors in the United States.[30]

But the challenges discussed in this chapter solidify the notion that we should do better. With better data, more careful estimation strategies, and clearer explanations of the strengths and weaknesses of available wage-by-major statistics, this data could become far more helpful to undergraduate students, millions of whom are presently making important college major decisions based on low-quality information about the long-run financial ramifications of their choices.

❼

Access to
Your Preferred Major

The metrics we have examined so far are sold, in one way or another, as consumer information. They're built on the idea that if only we gave prospective students better data, they could make better choices about their education.

But are students as free to make these choices as they think they are? This chapter examines one area where students may think they have that type of consumer choice but where many colleges have actually built a system that increasingly removes such choices by limiting the ability of students to select their preferred majors. At some public university campuses, budget pressures are also reducing students' access to other educational opportunities, including the ability to take courses outside their major and to study in classes small enough to permit conversations with professors.

In the popular imagination, students major in the field they think is the best fit for them, or one they have a passion for, or maybe just one that will prepare them for the job they want. But at many public universities, getting into that major is not so easy. Many high-demand majors require prospective students to prove themselves by earning high grades in specified introductory courses before they can declare the major. A student who does not make those grades is pushed to complete a different major—in many cases one that might interest them much less. Being ejected from many high-demand majors can also harm a student's career prospects. This claim may seem to contradict our advice in chapter 6 that you should not choose a major that does not interest you simply because other students who chose it ended up with higher earnings. However, there is no contradiction. In this chapter we are concerned with students who are interested in a particular major but are prevented from completing it. That is, we are interested in the effects of constraining a student's choices. And constraining the choice of a major *does* lower a student's future wages.[1]

More disturbing still, the students most likely to be prevented by these restrictions from selecting their first-choice major tend to be precisely those who need college the most: lower-income students and those from underrepresented racial groups. Major restrictions are particularly common in science, technology, engineering and math (STEM) fields and this work in opposition to efforts to ensure greater representation of people from these disadvantaged groups in those fields. Worse, these restrictions are particularly common at public universities, institutions that have an explicit mandate to promote equality of opportunity and whose students increasingly come from disadvantaged racial and economic groups.[2]

We will use the University of California, Santa Barbara (UCSB) to illustrate the problem. UCSB has risen in the national rankings while serving growing numbers of disadvantaged students under increasingly serious budgetary pressures. Learning conditions have deteriorated. Students are acutely aware of this and of rising costs and have flooded toward the majors whose students tend to get higher-wage jobs after graduating. Competition for entry has become stiff and students, especially those from disadvantaged backgrounds, are increasingly pushed out of their preferred majors. Many of them find themselves in majors that are associated with lower per-student spending on faculty and instruction, with more lenient grading standards, and with worse *average* employment outcomes. (But please remember what we told you in the last chapter—that the average wages earned by people who end up completing particular majors are probably not representative of what *you* are likely to earn in those majors.)

We draw on recent statistical research by two of our authors (Zachary Bleemer and Aashish Mehta) that shows how polices that restrict access to majors—sometimes referred to as "pre-majors" or "GPA caps"—have restricted the educational choices of disadvantaged students at UCSB and three other UC campuses. The mechanism is both intuitive and familiar: a selection policy that is usually set for practical and meritocratic reasons becomes a new way for those from more advantaged families to distinguish themselves from the less advantaged. SAT prep classes and Advanced Placement courses already play this role, for example. It is well established that such mechanisms play a major role in determining which students go to college and which colleges they go to.[3] It is hardly a stretch to see that similar mechanisms are likely to operate in similar ways within universities. Bleemer and Mehta's research shows that major restriction policies are particularly common at the most prestigious public universities, where they increasingly ration access to the highest-wage majors in racially inequitable ways.

Our unequivocal conclusion is that major restriction policies are bad for students. They make students jump through hoops, causing anxiety at a moment when they should be feeding their brains instead of worrying about which majors they should attempt to qualify for. They also do not direct students to the majors they would be relatively good at. Most important, they waste opportunities to use colleges' formidable capacity for turning students underserved by low-quality high school education into much more productive and secure adults.

How does all this relate to metrics? Essentially, this is a critical issue that is discreetly tucked out of sight by so many of the metrics students and families see. No ranking or other comparative database on universities reflects any information about major restrictions or their impact on the universities' upward mobility mission. This includes those that claim to report which universities do the most for that mission. Despite claims that "upward mobility" rankings and statistics provide transparency and hold universities accountable, they do not promote transparency about what students can *actually study*. Deteriorating learning conditions may not have obvious effects on rankings either. As a result, when it comes to working these things out, students are unfortunately on their own. Universities do not hide this information, but they don't advertise it either. Rather, this information has to be pieced together by students scouring multiple websites. We will therefore offer some tips on how to assess barriers to entry into majors and the learning conditions within majors. We will also discuss some ways to overcome these impediments to your education.

Social Mobility at College: A Case Study

Social mobility is the ability to escape the socioeconomic limitations imposed by one's family and racial background. Let's begin by looking at how social mobility outcomes and student major access have fared at UCSB over the past two decades and how those changes have been reflected in rankings and other information that is currently available to prospective students. Some of the authors of this book know the UCSB campus well, and that permits us to describe actual student experiences alongside facts and figures. It is also a representative case study of a prestigious public university: the mechanisms that are blocking mobility and student choice at UCSB are having similar effects at other prestigious public universities in the United States.[4]

In 2020, *U.S. News & World Report* ranked UCSB 7th in the nation among public universities, 34th among all national universities, and 9th among the "Top Performers for Social Mobility." In chapter 2, we discussed why general university rankings are not particularly useful. This UCSB case study will reveal what the *U.S. News* social mobility rankings are hiding. Those rankings are solely based on the proportion of Federal Pell Grant recipients who graduate from college within six years,[5] adjusted (in some unspecified way) to give more weight to campuses that host many Pell Grant recipients. The *U.S. News* data compares the graduation rates of those students to those of students who do not receive Pell Grants.

This is certainly useful information, as students who fail to graduate forfeit much of the economic payoff of attending college but are still responsible for paying back their student debt (many Pell Grant recipients nowadays also take out student loans). However, there are often significant differences by race and class in the academic opportunities available to students, even among those who do graduate. These differences in opportunities are not reflected in the *U.S. News* "Top Performers in Social Mobility" list or indeed in any college rankings that we know of.[6] And at UCSB those differences have grown.

The struggle to ensure equality of academic opportunity begins with students' personal finances. *U.S. News* ranks UCSB only 156th in the nation on "value for money," a measure that takes into account the net cost of attendance relative to the institution's assessed quality. The reasons for UCSB's relatively poor performance do not relate to the direct costs of college enrollment: because it is a public university, in-state tuition is subsidized and financial aid covers most tuition costs for working-class students. But students' scholarships do not generally cover living expenses, and Santa Barbara is a very expensive town to live in. Lower-income students struggle to handle these expenses, often in ways that net price calculators do not reflect.[7]

Students from less wealthy families routinely report that they make conscious choices in response to these concerns about cost and debt. These include decisions to work longer hours, forgo second majors, choose majors with low credit-unit requirements over those that they are interested in, and work longer hours than their course schedule allows. Some students skip class to work more hours and others commute fifty to one hundred miles or sleep in cars in order to avoid paying rent. They try to cram more than the required number of courses into a quarter and either forgo study-abroad programs or choose programs abroad that have lower costs.[8]

It was not always this way. California's legislature and governors of both parties have systematically cut the state's per-student contribution to University of California finances for over two decades. This resource squeeze came at a bad time for the university's mission of facilitating upward mobility. Undergraduate enrollment, which has accelerated sharply after being fairly stable in the 2000s,[9] now includes a larger share of less-advantaged students. The share of students from underrepresented minorities increased from 16% in 1999 to 29% in 2016. At the same time, by 2016, nearly half of the students came from families making less than $80,000 year.[10]

On paper then, the university needed more money to increase the number of residence halls, classrooms, and study spaces. And more low-income and minority students needed greater investments in student services, given that less well-connected students who are dealing with more complex and disruptive life circumstances usually require more academic advising, personal counseling, tutoring, emergency financial support, and career counseling.

What occurred was a compromise. Even as state funding collapsed, the University of California system increased its per-student spending in an effort to meet the needs of a more diverse and larger student body. That left the university no choice but to raise tuition.[11] The university mostly shielded low-income students from the brunt of this increase. It turned instead to out-of-state and international students, who pay higher tuition. But the conditions for instruction and learning undoubtedly suffered.

The deterioration in learning conditions is most obvious in class sizes. Detailed data collected by the University of California ClioMetric History Project permitted us to calculate these conditions in ways that accurately reflect student experience.[12] In 2000, the median class size for an average UCSB student across all the classes they took during their years at UCSB was 73 students. By 2016, this number had risen to 111. In 2000, 25% of the classes of the typical student had fewer than 30 students; by 2016, only 19% had fewer than 30 students. We chose this cutoff because with more than 30 students in a ten-week course, it is practically impossible for a professor to supervise individual project work.[13] These changes reflect not just increases in the number of students in the same courses but also reductions in some departments in the number of small courses that each faculty member can offer.

This deepening scarcity of pedagogical resources has increasingly limited students' opportunities to explore their intellectual horizons. Students began to report, especially in the wake of large increases in student numbers starting in 2010, that they were no longer able to enroll in classes outside their major they were interested in. This is because undergraduate advisors, whose job it is to schedule courses and help students graduate on time, have increasingly insisted on reserving seats in courses for students who require those courses for their major.[14] No doubt as a consequence of these pressures, the percentage of UCSB graduates who complete more than one major decreased from over 14% in 2004 to 9% in 2016. A damning article in the *Santa Barbara Independent* in 2021 reported that students were having a difficult time finding enough seats in courses to enroll in the 12 credit units required to qualify for financial aid. It quotes the dean of UCSB's College and Letters & Science, who describes the problem as one his office had seen coming but lacked the resources to prevent.[15]

And yet the same week that article appeared, *U.S. News* increased UCSB's ranking to 5th among public universities in the country. Of course it is possible, in theory, that intellectual options narrowed even faster at the other universities that compete with UCSB. A more plausible interpretation is that whatever the rankings reflect has very little to do with students' day-to-day educational opportunities.[16]

The Big Shakeout

This is the environment in which growing numbers of disadvantaged students at UCSB seek upward mobility through college education. Unfortunately, scarcity tends to breed competition, and competition does not usually favor the less prepared. Acing a physical chemistry exam is much more difficult for students who didn't study calculus or have access to a chemistry lab in high school. Doing it while waiting tables twenty hours a week is even harder.

We chose chemistry as our example for a reason. Interest in STEM fields has grown significantly over the past twelve to fifteen years. A series of reports by the National Academy of Sciences, the National Academy of Engineering, and the Institute of Medicine warned of dire consequences if STEM skill gaps were not filled, and STEM mania accelerated during the years of weak labor markets that followed the 2008 financial crisis.[17]

The number of bachelor's degrees in science and engineering fields boomed at UCSB (as was the case across the country) but decreased abruptly starting with the class of 2011 (fig. 7.1). In part, this number climbed before 2011 because of growing student anxiety about perceived differences in the employment benefits of different majors (see Chapter 6 for a primer on why these differences are likely to be overestimates). Probably for the same reasons, the number of humanities graduates declined after the 2008 financial crisis. While it is difficult to prove precisely why the STEM numbers fell after 2011, it is widely thought that departments that house some of the high-demand majors used competitive pre-majors more deliberately to deflect the large influx of new students. Perhaps as a consequence, the number of social sciences graduates increased significantly.

So how did underrepresented minorities (URMs) and lower-income students fare in this shakeout? The proportion of students from

FIGURE 7.1.

UCSB undergraduate degrees by broad division, 1995–2015

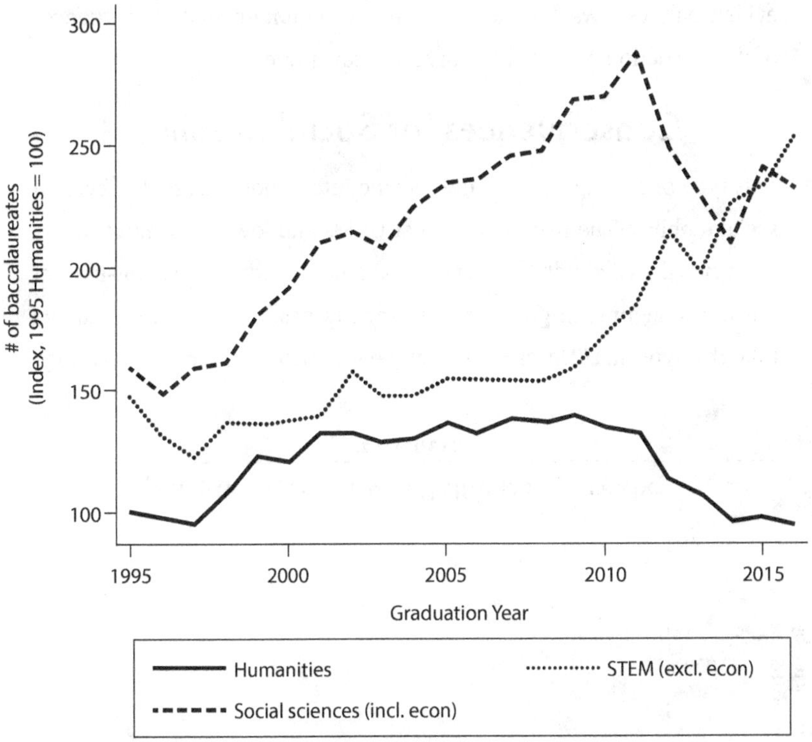

Source: UCSB Planning and Databook, online database, accessed July 2019.

those groups has always been lower in STEM fields than in the humanities and social sciences. The underrepresentation of women and certain minority students in the sciences has been a widely discussed problem among policy makers for some time, so some improvements in minority representation might have been expected. However, the gap did not close at UCSB. In 2005, URMs made up just 10% of STEM majors and 14% in the other majors.[18] Their share of STEM majors increased to 22% by 2016, but their share of non-STEM majors increased much more, to 36%. These results, together with the absence of any evidence that lower-income and URM students are less interested in STEM fields, suggest that the sorting is not voluntary. Indeed, we will soon provide evidence that shows that these outcomes were unintended consequences of the restriction policies the university sanctioned.

Consequences for Social Mobility

This type of sorting by race and income into majors has real effects on social mobility. The first effect is that URMs and lower-income students are increasingly completing majors that tend to offer worse labor-market outcomes. Figure 7.2 graphs the average wages by major of the majors that the typical URM student completed each year and the average

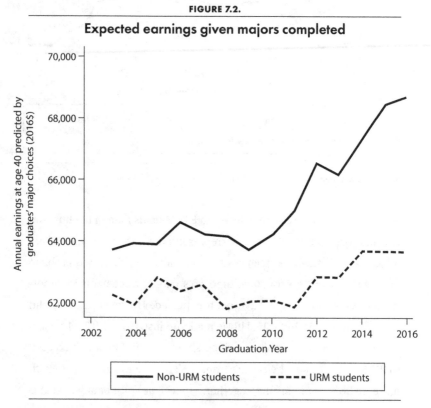

FIGURE 7.2.

Expected earnings given majors completed

Source: Authors' calculations from American Community Survey data.

wages of those that other students tended to complete for the period 2002–2016. The wage associated with any given major is assumed to be the same for both groups; all that is permitted to differ between the groups is the fraction of students who actually accessed the higher- and lower-wage majors.[19] The gap between the groups grew from roughly 3% of earnings in 2003 to around 8% in 2016. It can be similarly shown that, again relative to other students, URM students are increasingly graduating from majors associated with lower employment rates.[20]

The second effect is that the majors that serve URMs and low-income students receive fewer pedagogical resources. Repeating the analysis in figure 7.2 but this time replacing the wages associated with each major with the major's instructional budget per student shows that by 2016, the departments that host the likely majors of underrepresented students were given around 11% less money to spend on instruction per credit unit than the departments of majors that other students typically enrolled in. This difference in per-student instructional expenditures between the majors completed by these two groups of students did not exist in 2003.

The third effect on social mobility of increasing student stratification across majors concerns departments' average grades. Figure 7.3 plots the typical grades in courses offered in each department against the percentage of students that department graduated in the academic year 2016–2017 who belong to underrepresented racial groups (the graph on the left) or are from low-income families (the graph on the right). The upward sloping lines clearly indicate that the departments that serve more disadvantaged students tended to offer much higher grades. This sorting of students by ethnicity and income into relatively grade-inflated majors has also become worse over time. As veteran instructors, we know that even the most well-meaning students will put less time and effort into our courses if high grades are readily available. Peer-reviewed studies concur that grade inflation significantly reduces student effort.[21] It follows that disadvantaged students are, on

FIGURE 7.3.

Average median 2017 UCSB course grades by department and by department share of URM and low-income students

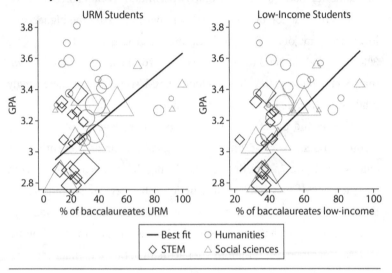

Note: Each observation is a department. The size of the marker captures the number of 2016–17 graduates completing that major. See figure 7.4 for source note.

average, receiving a less demanding education than other students and that this difference has grown.[22]

To be clear, we are not arguing that faculty who teach in majors that serve more URMs take their teaching less seriously than those who teach in majors who serve fewer URMs. What differs are the strategies available to preserve research time. Majors that serve fewer URMs tend to have pre-majors and the faculty who teach them tend to rely on less-qualitative exercises that can be graded entirely by machines or by teaching assistants to reduce grading time per student. They often using tougher grading and the pre-major itself to control the number of students. Instructors in majors who serve more URMs and in typically unrestricted majors tend to teach qualitative material that is graded subjectively, and lenient grading in this context reduces the time students seeking feedback demand.

Inequality of Opportunity?

All we have shown so far is that students from differing backgrounds end up having increasingly dissimilar educational experiences on the same campus. To understand whether gaps in educational opportunities have grown, one has to understand why this has happened.[23] We will show you that for a large and growing number of students, this is not a choice.

Let's begin by ruling out one possible explanation: declines in the relative academic preparation of URM and low-income students. Figure 7.4 provides the SAT scores of URM, low-income, and all UCSB graduates by the year they graduated. It shows that the disadvantaged students' scores are lower than the campus average but that they have risen significantly and just as fast as those of non-URM and wealthier students. Gaps in average SAT scores between lower-income students and average scores for the entire campus have closed since the financial crisis. Preparation gaps therefore are therefore unlikely to account for growing inequality of outcome. As it happens, URM and lower-income students today are *more* capable on average of succeeding in the most-sought-after majors than they were in the past.

Our research shows that major restriction policies are a likely culprit. They tend to be imposed in the majors most in demand as a means of controlling student enrollment and in technical majors that feature course material that is difficult to master without certain foundational skill sets. For both of these reasons, the most frequently restricted majors are in STEM disciplines and business.

In research into the effects of restrictions on four UC campuses, Bleemer and Mehta showed that pre-majors filter out URM and lower-income students more aggressively than students who are not URMs and students who do not come from low-income families. They also showed that this happens mostly because restrictions make it increasingly difficult for students with weaker high school backgrounds to

FIGURE 7.4.

Average SAT/ACT score by student group at UC Santa Barbara, 2002–2016

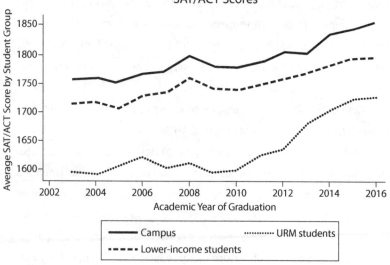

Note: Dataset includes only students who completed all four years at UC Santa Barbara.

Source: Authors' calculations from UCSB student records in Zachary Bleemer, "The UC ClioMetric History Project and Formatted Optical Character Recognition," Center for Studies in Higher Education Research and Occasional Papers 18, no. 3, 2018, https://cshe.berkeley .edu/publications/uc-cliometric-history-project-and-formatted-optical-character-recognition -zachary.

qualify for access to restricted majors. Restricting a major substantially decreases the likelihood that students with lower SAT scores and first-year GPAs will be able to study in that department.[24]

Bleemer and Mehta examined these effects with a detailed case study that focused on entry into the economics majors at UCSB and UC Davis in the period 2010–2016. The student bodies at the two campuses are broadly similar. The economics department at UCSB had policies that restricted access to its majors throughout that period but UC Davis did not. Patterns of major declaration at UC Davis therefore provide a sense of how students' preferences for economics vary by gender, race, and class. If these patterns are different at UCSB, the differences are likely to be the effects of a major restriction. The evidence suggests that restrictions have several effects that a prospective college student should care about.

First: restrictions make it less likely that students interested in a major will be able to access it. For example, students who take Economics 1 are much less likely to complete an economics major at UCSB than they are at UC Davis.[25] Second: this lack of access is more pronounced among students from URM groups or lower-income families. The income and racial differences in the probability of declaring an economics major are much larger at UCSB than at Davis, even though there is no evidence that racial and income differences in interest in the subject differ on these two campuses. Finally, this happens because of differences in prior preparation: students who attended a private high school, took Advanced Placement or international baccalaureate economics courses in high school, and scored well on the SATs have a better chance of obtaining good grades in required courses and thus a better chance of qualifying for an economics major at UCSB.

The data also show what any rational observer should expect given how major restrictions are designed: they do not help match students to the majors that best suit them. Imagine that a student brimming with scientific potential who attended a weak high school is trying to determine whether she is likely to become a better chemist or a better historian by the time she graduates. Under the current system, she may never get to find out. She is likely to be ejected from the chemistry major after getting low grades in some first-year chemistry courses because she has not yet been able to make up for gaps in her prior training. The only thing she would learn about her potential in the two fields from this experience is that her high school did not prepare her well for introductory math and science courses.

And this brings us to the last point about restrictions: the students they reject are often pushed onto lower-earning career paths. Bleemer and Mehta have shown that UC Santa Cruz students who were interested in studying economics but were unable to do so because of the major restriction had 46% lower earnings two to six years after graduating than those who were not pushed out of the major.[26] In short, major restrictions are effective at pushing students out of their first-choice majors, they often reduce the expected earnings of displaced students, they are more likely to displace disadvantaged students, and they don't do a good job of matching students to the majors that suit them.

Unfortunately, major restrictions are increasingly common at colleges and universities. Most of schools on the *U.S. News* list of the top 25 public universities in the United States currently restrict entry to many of the majors that associated with the most lucrative careers: 13 have restrictions in computer science, 10 have them in economics, 23 restrict access to finance or business degrees, 24 restrict access to mechanical engineering programs, and every school that offered a nursing degree restricted entry to that major. Unfortunately, this information usually hasn't been collected in one place by individual universities, let alone across schools. The only way we were able to find this information was to go to the website of each department at each university and find their rules for declaring the major.

Major restrictions are administrative mechanisms for allocating opportunities and they are clearly contributing to inequality of opportunity. But prospective students should also be aware that departments have other ways of restricting access that can lead to inequality of outcome. A high course load early on in the major can discourage students with weak time-management skills or students who must work longer hours for pay. Large or growing differences in grading standards across majors can incentivize students to sort themselves out of a field even in the absence of a major restriction threshold.[27] And long sequences of required courses can make it harder for students who need to graduate on time to opt in to some majors later in their college careers, even if students are not required to make particular grades in these courses. Whatever the cause, university students should be aware that they may need or want to switch majors for reasons that have little to do with their interests and aptitudes.

Conclusion

The evidence reviewed in this chapter demonstrates that even specialized "economic mobility" university rankings do not accurately reflect much of the pedagogical experience available to students at different universities. This is particularly true for students from disadvantaged backgrounds. Some college rankings do take graduation rates among URM students and Pell Grant recipients into account. It is very helpful to know whether URM and students from lower-income families tend to graduate, and we strongly recommend that prospective students examine these data directly.[28] Unfortunately, these statistics can be managed by universities that offer majors that are easy to complete to keep their graduation rates high and then reserve the highest-demand majors for better-prepared students.[29] Moreover, rankings do not inform prospective students about serious barriers to entry they may have to overcome after they are admitted to a university in order to access many of its most popular majors or about the class sizes and other educational opportunities available in those majors. The rankings thus omit an important piece of the student experience and say little about racial and class inequality among students who do graduate.

We have made these points using the case study of UC Santa Barbara, a university that has risen in the rankings on other strengths even as classes have become more crowded, students' freedom to enroll in courses outside their major has declined, and the educational choices available to disadvantaged students appear to have diminished relative to those available to other students. This appears to be the natural consequence of several interrelated national trends, all of which afflict public universities nationwide: growing student numbers that coincide with decreasing per-student support from states, increasing reliance on tuition as a source of revenue, a fixation on rankings that leads administrators to ignore other priorities, and a preference for STEM fields that is exacerbated by anxieties produced by rising student debt loads. These trends have resulted in surges of student interest that departments cannot handle. Departments then solve the issue by making policies that restrict access to majors in high demand. Unfortunately, those policies give an advantage to students with the best prior preparation, not necessarily those with the most to gain from studying the subject, and this generates serious social stratification and limits educational opportunities—and particularly those of already-disadvantaged students.

So what is a prospective university student to do? The standard metrics do not help and the ones you need are not published. Before deciding whether a particular college makes sense for you, it is important to make extensive inquiries about the pathways into your preferred majors and about the learning conditions once you get in.

Departments that attempt to filter out students are usually transparent about their rules for declaring the major on their website because this makes possible an even-handed and less time-consuming application of the rules. Some also hope that transparency about restrictions may encourage some students to opt out from the start. You should find the departments that host the majors you want to complete and examine the requirements and procedures for declaring the major.

You should also examine the university's course schedule for recent terms. This information is usually available online. Examine class sizes, which often vary enormously across majors within the same campus. Take notes on the class sizes in both required courses and electives in your target major. If the electives are all too large to allow for direct contact with professors (30–40 is the threshold in our experience), then it is more likely that a graduate teaching assistant will be reviewing your work and answering your questions. Many teaching assistants are superb instructors, but professors usually have greater subject expertise. If you have your heart set on a particular major at a particular university, you might even want to review recent course syllabi to see if the classes include substantial amounts of project-based learning.

After learning about these rules and learning conditions, you should contact staff in interesting departments whose job it is to advise students and help them navigate academic requirements. Ask about specific issues that matter to you. The rules are written by professors, but it is the staff that must implement them, and they often try to interpret them in ways that will help students graduate on time. They are therefore great sources of useful information and suggestions. For example, you might ask them whether an Advanced Placement or community college course you have taken could be used for college credit, whether you can take two required courses at the same time instead of in sequence, or how easy it is for students in the department to double major.

We hope that by gathering this information you will be able to make informed choices about which college to attend and how you can get the most out of the education it offers.

Conclusion

Metrics and Waste

> Let us love what is beautiful when we see it, without bothering
> about weighing it. Let us repay the enthusiasm of talent with the
> enthusiasm of esteem; and leave the scales to the merchants.
> —Jean-François Sobry (1743–1820)

Students and their families are surrounded by a cacophony of metrics as they make important decisions about college (see Table C.1). Taken together, our chapters have given you tools to help you see through familiar but faulty numbers and put better numbers in the context of your personal background, preferences, and goals. If you want to use metrics to help you make important decisions about where to go to college and what to study while you're there, though, it's also important that you understand where quantitative metrics come from and why they are so prevalent. To that end, we want to end this book by explaining some of the reasons we think so many metrics remain popular, even if they are (sometimes terminally) flawed. We also want to explain why there is so much hype surrounding the metrics discussed in each of the previous chapters and to highlight how this hype is causing problems for universities, students, and—most pressingly—for democracy.

Metrics are all about simplification. They clear away context and complexity, often replacing hundreds or thousands of conflicting assessments with a single number. This simplification can be useful. After all, sometimes we just need to know how many apples are in a basket instead of knowing every detail about each apple. But in many impor-

TABLE C.1.

Summary of college metrics

STANDARD METRIC	BETTER MEASUREMENT
Return on investment	Your personal goals
Rankings	Graduation rates
Selectivity	Instructional spending per student
Tuition sticker price	Net cost to you
Individual debt	Mutual obligations
Wages by major	Better wage-by-major statistics
Social mobility ranking	Access to your first-choice major

tant ways, universities are not like apples and neither are students. Universities and colleges are diverse institutions in diverse places with different guiding principles, different teaching models, and different understandings of student achievement. Students have different backgrounds, goals, and visions of the future. Metrics can be useful, but you should be careful to not be seduced by their simplicity.

Some metrics are popular because interested parties stand to benefit when you pay attention to them. As we discussed in chapter 1, PayScale directly benefits when you engage with its return-on-investment metrics. Like many other digital platforms, it depends on collecting data from users to produce its metrics. The entities that produce the most popular *U.S. News* or *Times Higher Education* university rankings that we discussed in chapter 2 are private, for-profit companies that depend on the widespread use of their rankings to sell advertising. If no one paid attention to their rankings they would go out of business, so even though their metrics are flawed, they work hard to encourage you to use them. In some cases, the popularity of those flawed metrics has more to do with momentum and marketing by powerful interests than it does with the distribution of useful information, and you should view them with a skeptical eye.

But being a skeptical consumer of metrics is just the beginning. Metrics are also changing the very nature of higher education in ways we think are damaging. Critics of higher education often allege that universities are wasteful and that metrics are a way to measure universities and make them more efficient. We disagree. Often what creates waste is bad quantitative metrics and the narrow vision that accompanies them. We might say that quantitative metrics are *wasting the university*, but we don't mean to imply that they are turning universities into trash. We mean that metrics are helping turn the university into something that no longer serves the functions that most members of society want them to serve.

Emulating Intelligence

Let's begin with one of the fiercest historical critics of universities, the economist and anthropologist Thorstein Veblen. More than 100 years ago, Veblen began observing what he called "conspicuous consumption" and "pecuniary emulation" in American society: the tendency of certain classes of people, especially the upper classes, to demonstrate their social status by buying expensive things. Veblen observed that many people lower on the social scale were spending money in an effort to mimic those above if they could afford to do so. He called this phenomenon waste because he thought that this "competitive consumption" did little to make people happier and may in fact have damaged society by misusing, or wasting, resources.

In the final chapter of his book *The Theory of the Leisure Class*, published in 1899, Veblen described the wasteful activities of the universities of his time. He was particularly interested in the spectacles that marked important university events—such as cap-and-gown ceremonies—which he saw as attempts to reinvigorate the "priestly" and even "magical" aspects of "archaic" universities. He also called out elite universities' snobbish disdain of education in "merely useful" knowledge, such as technical and scientific classes designed to provide students with skills needed for industry and innovation. Upper-class college students preferred to spend their time taking classes in the arts, humanities, and "classics," which he characterized as knowledge without any obvious material application.[1] Veblen wrote that upper-class students' pursuit of the arts and humanities was wasteful in light of what the industrial economy demanded of them. In other words, even though Veblen placed great value on the arts and humanities, he observed that many of the students enrolled in these subjects, especially at prestigious universities, took these courses just to demonstrate that they had the wherewithal to "waste" their time by ignoring the practical skills that an industrial economy required.

Veblen saved his most cutting criticism for *The Higher Learning in America*, published twenty years later. The book's overarching critique was that universities were being overrun by businesspeople and the competitive logic of the free market. Veblen railed against universities' attempts to emulate for-profit businesses by striving for mindless efficiency, encouraging drastic increases in undergraduate enrollment, and constructing hierarchical bureaucracies to manage the university's professors. He even criticized university sports teams as an attempt to advertise and build prestige, which he argued diverted attention and resources from the vital functions of the university. He made a similar argument about "pomp and circumstance" ceremonies, which he claimed were little more than "expedients of advertising."[2]

Quantitative metrics like the ones described in our book did not escape Veblen's attention. He was keenly aware of the role of statistical measurements, especially those used in the management of undergraduate teaching, where he noted attempts to pay instructors for each individual unit of teaching completed, similar to how factory workers were paid by the piece rather than for each hour of work. Veblen saw all of this as proof that a competitive corporate ethos dominated universities that encouraged students and academics to focus on surface appearances instead of on open inquiry and deep comprehension.

Veblen's analysis was eerily prescient. Metrics-focused competition often distracts universities from their job of providing a high-quality education and producing excellent research. Public funding is increasingly being replaced by private tuition at public colleges, as we discussed in chapter 5. Universities compete for students by attempting to boost their scores on various rankings. Administrative bureaucracies have exploded in size and influence partly as a result of these changes.

But before returning to metrics in today's universities, we want to point out three things about Veblen's understanding of waste. The first is that the universities of Veblen's day were being overtaken by a class of industrial managers who, along with their bureaucratic assistants, were attempting to turn higher learning into a competitive and efficient enterprise. Businesspeople of the day criticized universities that were managed by professors as inefficient and wasteful because they too often ignored financial concerns, were uninterested in growing the industrial economy, and did not place enough emphasis on training students for industrial work.

Second, in their efforts to transform the university into an institution that focused on the bottom line, managers relied on metrics that made the world of inquiry and teaching measurable, thus promoting "tangible efficiency."[3] This included systems for measuring things such as teaching and learning credits. Veblen pointed out that these trackable statistics allowed administrators to control aspects of the university, but they explained little about the pursuit of knowledge. He also emphasized the tremendous work required to establish and maintain this system of appearances on the part of students, professors, and the growing bureaucracy.

Third, Veblen was not interested in a nostalgic attempt to save a sacred version of the university. Rather, he was concerned with the influence of the business world on the university, and he was attempting to understand and make sense of the transformation of universities as part of a broader society that was increasingly influenced by industry. He observed that open-ended scholarship and inquiry and the high-quality teaching that depended on such scholarship were being consumed by activities that could be measured with money.

Emulating Private Goods

This is not the place to present a thorough history of universities from Veblen's time up to the present day, but we do want to briefly consider some changes that began in the 1970s. After World War II, universities were crucial for Cold War research and development, which made them highly dependent on federal grants that were expected to drive innovations that would be useful to the defense industry.[4] At the same time, between World War II and 1970—a period of significant growth and expansion—public universities were meant to do more than just generate economic growth; they were also institutions that promoted a learned democratic society.[5] In other words, public universities and the services they provided were public goods, a form of collective wealth that benefited everyone, not just individual students.[6] Part of the mission of many public institutions was to assist the private sector by supporting and contributing to technological progress and helping students acquire the skills they needed to get good jobs, but these were not the only or even the primary reasons for the existence of universities.

This began to change in the 1970s.[7] A competitive ethos made it more difficult to justify and maintain public goods. Because they were not subject to market forces or formal competition, many people began to see public goods as a waste of public resources. For prominent economists of the period such as Milton Friedman and Gary Becker, public goods came to be seen as an frontier for the development of private property and market transactions.

Put differently, many officials saw public goods as wasteful because they appeared to lack the rational ordering that free markets presumably provide, and these officials saw this as evidence that they were inefficient. They assumed that subjecting public goods such as research and civic knowledge to market forces would distribute them more efficiently. This tendency to "privatize" public goods also drew on older ideas. The English philosopher John Locke argued that people laboring on common lands was the origin of private property. Human labor "improved" the land and transformed it from something worthless (or what later became known in Britain as "the wastes") into something productive, marketable, and thus valuable.[8] We can see some parallels here: just as the transition from feudalism to capitalism pushed former inhabitants of common land to form a "labor market" and accept industrial employment, today's tech companies capture and enclose publicly available data that they then sell in new marketplaces. The enclosure of universities behind "walls" of selectivity and high tuition prices creates new markets that allocate newly scarce educational resources to student "consumers." Metrics facilitate and even encourage these enclosures of common educational goods.

To sum all of this up: today, many people believe that universities—especially public universities—are wasteful because they are sheltered from the competitive pressures of the free market that they believe will increase educational "efficiency."[9] Quantitative metrics facilitate this understanding of universities as a contemporary version of "the wastes, something to be enclosed or improved." The same officials and citizens who believe that higher education is crucial for developing the economy, creating technological innovations, and creating a pool of highly skilled workers also tend to think that universities are unmanageable and underdeveloped. Metrics such as average wages by major and return on investment are a step in the direction of competitively disciplining universities, but they still don't sufficiently translate universities' outputs into the profit and yield measures of banking and finance.

Those same people often see universities as failing to provide a proper accounting of their public resources. Just how many units of useful knowledge did that political science class generate for each dollar of taxpayer money it received? For many, the solution is to subject universities to various market forces and maybe even turn them into private corporations that are exclusively concerned with producing private benefits. A crucial step in this process is to measure everything related to university production in numerical terms, to make them literally accountable. Measuring public universities and what they produce in quantitative terms is the beginning of the process of changing public goods into private and marketable commodities.

Transforming public universities into quasi-private institutions that compete for resources, focus on serving customers, and produce the conditions for economic development is not easy. One of this book's authors, Chris Newfield, has shown that privatizing universities—in the sense of shifting universities' revenue from public block grants to private tuition—has driven down the quality of college instruction and has harmed students and researchers by increasing administrative costs and creating substantial new expenses.[10] This turns the argument that public universities are wasteful on its head. Turning universities into competitive, economic institutions that are always focused on the bottom line is the more truly wasteful act because it diverts resources from the basic functions of a university: quality instruction and open-ended inquiry (research).

Creating crude metrics and quantitative benchmarks for all sorts of goods and services requires deliberative work. But as Veblen pointed out 100 years ago, the assumptions that allow things to be compared quantitatively—especially things such as learning that are difficult to measure—are often flawed, and the resulting available statistics often have a dubious relationship with underlying daily practices and actual outcomes. University administrators are aware of this problem and are hiring more and more people to reduce the difference between the measurements and actual practice. This very expensive work helps explain the massive increase in administrative staff over the last forty years.[11]

Wasting Emulation

Every university is different, but the many universities that the five authors of this book have attended and taught at are all institutions that give more than they take. Another way to think about this is that the impact of universities goes beyond what can be measured. But as society increasingly relies on simplistic measures to make sense of universities, things that cannot easily be measured become less important. Some resources have absolute limits, of course, and it makes sense to count and assess them in simplistic ways. But many do not. Markets and the array of metrics that accompany them treat abundant educational resources as lacking in value and "going to waste." In many settings, the university is increasingly dominated by what the geographer Marcus Doel calls "miserly thinking."[12] This corporate management mindset limits the scope of universities by thinking of them as scarce resources that are subject to competition and that can (and must) be measured and managed as such.

Public universities are not perfect. For example, they have not done a good enough job of providing benefits to marginalized people. For this and other reasons, universities should be accountable for the public money they spend. But decontextualized metrics are generally not the best way to accomplish this accountability.

Why? For one thing, there is always a danger that performance metrics will take on a life of their own. This is captured by Goodhart's law, which states that when measures of performance become *targets for* performance, they no longer operate as useful measures.[13] This isn't a problem in the case of something like baseball, where the goal of the game (winning) is defined by a simple metric (which team gets the most runs). As a result, runs are simultaneously a target for baseball teams and an important measure of success of a team. But higher education is not a game and its outputs are much more challenging to measure than runs in a baseball game. As universities are increasingly judged by their graduates' future wages, they are increasingly reorganizing themselves to produce high-wage graduates. But this means that things that cannot be measured in relation to students' future wages or things that can be measured but are not seen as something that contributes to high wages are at a greater risk of funding cuts or elimination. Many of these things, including small seminars suitable for deep discussion, cultural events, and individual discussions with professors about questions a student has pondered for a long time, are the best-remembered and most transformative components of a person's college experience.

"Bibliometrics," a set of metrics that rank academic research and journals, provide an example of how Goodhart's law plays out in universities.[14] Bibliometrics were originally designed as tools librarians could use to make decisions about what academic publications to buy. But they have evolved into a way to judge the value of the academic research of individual professors. They have become a target that influences publication decisions professors make and which research questions they pursue. One of this book's authors recently received an email from a university administrator praising publications that were cited in other publications many times and urging researchers to stop writing articles and chapters that will be only rarely cited in the work of other academics. The email completely disregarded whether research topics would be interesting to students or the broader nonacademic world. The administrator directed the recipients to the publishing company Elsevier's newest bibliometric tool, which everyone could use to "self-reflect on your own future publications strategy." This kind of narrow thinking, which relies exclusively on a set of metrics that leaves out much of what is valuable about scientific and humanistic research, explicitly damages openness and freedom of inquiry and may ultimately hinder the capacity of universities to change the world for the better.

For us, this is the real tragedy of wastefulness in universities. By attempting to capture, measure, and compete for every aspect of higher education, we are causing the deterioration of the broad and immeasurable benefits of attentive teaching and open inquiry at a time when society desperately needs them. This is doing real and lasting—but completely unnecessary—damage to the public university.

We wrote this book to help you see the many problems with standard college metrics and become a sophisticated, self-reflective user of them. But in this conclusion, we've asked you to consider a further step—to question the miserly thinking that drives governments, funding agencies, universities, and researchers to treat education and research as a scarce resource that requires incessant, flawed, and misdirected measurement and that drives students to ill-constructed metrics to help guide some of their life's most important decisions. Instead, if we can come to see the university's core functions of creating and disseminating knowledge as more than a matter of economic scarcity, we will be able to reinvigorate what Veblen referred to as the "cult of learning" that is central to an enlightened society. We've shown how college applicants can make a better use of metrics and, just as important, how they can decide when to set metrics aside. Better—and more restricted—uses of metrics can help everyone have a better experience of the widespread benefits of higher education.

Acknowledgments

This book was conceived during a three-month 2018 residential research fellowship at the University of California Humanities Research Institute (UCHRI) called "The Limits of the Numerical: Metrics and the Humanities in Higher Education," convened by Christopher Newfield. We owe thanks to David Theo Goldberg, who saw the potential in the project, and to Kelly Anne Brown and the tremendous UCHRI staff, including Suedine Nakano, Arielle Read, Yolanda Choo, and Beth Greene. The UCHRI's residential research groups support collaborative work in the humanities of a type that is all too rare and is financially endangered everywhere. We hope its model continues to expand.

We are particularly grateful to Heather Steffen and Laura Mandell, who also participated in the fellowship group and provided foundational ideas and extremely helpful feedback throughout the project. Heather was an organizational stalwart and inspiration from start to finish.

We are also grateful to part-time participants Gabriele Badano, Greg Lusk, and Liz Chatterjee, friends and colleagues from the Cambridge and Chicago branches of the international Limits of the Numerical research project. The seminar was also enlarged and deepened by invited visitors who gave presentations and discussed our overlapping issues at length: thanks to Eric Archambault, Wendy Brown, Wendy Espeland, and Radhika Gorur for their thinking and feedback. Members of the University of California, Irvine faculty were also supportive and insightful. We are particularly grateful for discussions with Richard Arum, Annie McClanahan, and Kavita Philip.

The underlying research on the limits of the numerical in higher education was funded by National Endowment for the Humanities Collaborative Research Grant RZ-255780-17. It also received timely support from John Majewski, dean of humanities and fine arts at the University of California Santa Barbara. Thanks also to several units for publication support: Dean of Social Sciences Charles Hale at UC Santa Barbara, the Office of Research at UC Irvine, the Center for the Study of Higher Education at UC Berkeley, Swansea University in Wales, and the Independent Social Research Foundation in London. The grants and all UC Santa Barbara events were administered by its Chicano Studies Institute, where we were helped by Marcelina Ortiz and Tracey Goss. In addition to complicated accounting, Tracey managed a full range of negotiations and arrangements with vendors and UC Santa Barbara support units with a stamina and finesse that made everything easier and contributed materially to the final product. We are also indebted to Maya Bernal, Yuri Jeon, Alia Roca-Lezra, and especially Xina Soleri for invaluable research support. In addition, we would like to thank the participants in a May 2019 UC Santa Barbara conference, "Disquantified," who also helped develop our thinking.

We wrote this five-authored book to leverage our respective expertise in explaining the usefulness and effects of popular university metrics. We sought a comprehensive and integrated view. This meant that each chapter required working toward consensus, which we think substantially improved the book's quality as a whole. Each chapter also had a lead author. Zachary Bleemer was the lead on the chapters on university rankings, tuition sticker price, and average wages by college major. Mukul Kumar was the lead author of the return on investment chapter, and Aashish Mehta was the lead author on the chapter about access to preferred majors. Chris Muellerleile was the lead author on the student debt chapter and the conclusion, and Christopher Newfield was the lead author of the introduction and the chapter on selectivity. Each of us worked on all of the chapters, often multiple times, and we edited the continuous manuscript together in a series of memorable morning Zoom meetings in April 2020. We very much appreciated the comments of two anonymous referees of the manuscript. And we are grateful for the editorial work of Scott Smallwood, who edited the entire manuscript prior to final submission to Johns Hopkins University Press.

Academia is at its best when it brings collective intelligence to bear on a complicated set of problems, and we are thankful for the multiple types of institutional support we received.

Notes

Introduction

1. For the FBI affidavit about Operation Varsity Blues, see Laura Smith, "Affidavit in Support of Criminal Complaint," https://www.justice.gov/file /1142876/download. For the definitive account of the scandal, see Melissa Korn and Jennifer Levitz, *Unacceptable: Privilege, Deceit & the Making of the College Admissions Scandal* (New York: Portfolio/Penguin, 2020).

2. See, for example, Matt Feeney, "The Pointless End of Legacy Admissions," *The New Yorker*, November 23, 2021, https://www.newyorker.com/culture/cultural -comment/the-pointless-end-of-legacy-admissions.

Chapter 1. Return on Investment

1. White House, Office of the Press Secretary, "Remarks by the President on Opportunity for All and Skills for America's Workers," Waukesha, Wisconsin, January 30, 2014, https://obamawhitehouse.archives.gov/the-press-office/2014 /01/30/remarks-president-opportunity-all-and-skills-americas-workers.

2. Quoted in Scott Jaschik, "Apology from Obama," *Inside Higher Ed*, February 19, 2014, https://www.insidehighered.com/news/2014/02/19 /professor-art-history-receives-handwritten-apology-president-obama.

3. For an analysis of these trends within the context of public universities, see Christopher Newfield, *The Great Mistake: How We Wrecked Public Universities and How We Can Fix Them* (Baltimore: Johns Hopkins University Press, 2016).

4. Zachary First, "When the Humanities Are Worth It," PayScale, November 11, 2016, https://www.payscale.com/career-news/2016/11/what-major -should-i-choose.

5. ROI models that suffer from selection bias offer misleading data because they rely on nonrandomized samples that are not representative of the broader population. For a discussion of the effect of sample selection bias on educational outcomes such as earnings, see Richard Breen, Seongsoo Choi, Anders Holmb,

"Heterogeneous Causal Effects and Sample Selection Bias," *Sociological Science* 2 (2016): 351–369.

6. "9 Problems with Payscale.com's College Rankings," Around Learning: The Policy and Possibilities of Education, September 17, 2013, http:// aroundlearning.com/2013/09/8-problems-with-payscale-coms-college-rankings -and-one-solution/.

7. Anthony Carnevale, Ban Cheah, and Martin Van Der Werf, *A First Try at ROI: Ranking 4,500 Colleges* (Washington, DC: Georgetown University Center on Education and the Workforce, 2019).

8. Quoted in Rick Seltzer, "Return on Students' Investments Varies over Time," *Insider Higher Ed*, November 14, 2019, https://www.insidehighered.com /news/2019/11/14/differences-college-roi-vary-institution-type-and-time-frame -measured-report-says, our emphasis.

9. "PayScale 2017 ROI Report: Methodology and Notes," https://www .payscale.com/college-roi/methodology.

10. "How Money Ranked the 2019 Best Colleges," *Money*, n.d., https:// money.com/how-money-ranks-best-colleges-2019/.

11. Kim Clark, "How Money Ranked the 2016 Best Colleges," *Money*, July 11, 2016, https://money.com/how-money-ranks-best-colleges-2016/.

12. HoonHo Kim and Diane Lalancette, *Literature Review on the Value-Added Measurement in Higher Education* (Paris: Organisation for Economic Co-operation and Development, 2013).

13. For its 2022 Best College Rankings, Money shifted from PayScale to College Scorecard data. See "How Money Ranked the Best 2022 Best Colleges," *Money*, https://money.com/best-colleges/methodology/. See also "U.S. News and World Report Selects PayScale to Provide Alumni Salary Information for Its Popular Best Colleges Rankings Report," PayScale, September 11, 2017, https:// www.payscale.com/press-releases/u-s-news-world-report-selects-payscale-provide- alumni-salary-information-popular-best-colleges-rankings-report/; Forbes, "How We Rank America's Top Colleges," August 30, 2022, https://www.forbes.com/ sites/emmawhitford/2022/08/30/how-we-rank-americas-top-colleges/.

14. John Bound Charles Brown, and Nancy Mathiowetz, "Measurement Error in Survey Data," *Handbook of Econometrics* 5 (2001): 3705–3843.

15. "Website Terms of Use," PayScale, last updated May 11, 2018, https:// www.payscale.com/license.

16. "By providing or posting any User Content, you hereby automatically grant us an irrevocable, perpetual, royalty-free, non-exclusive, fully paid, sublicensable (through multiple tiers), and worldwide permission, right (including, any moral rights), and license to use, access, copy, perform, store, display, delete, distribute, modify, and otherwise process such User Content and to create derivative works of, or incorporate into other works, such User Content, and to grant and authorize sublicenses thereof"; "Website Terms of Use."

17. Students and their families should also know that PayScale is not a neutral arbiter of the value of a college degree. In fact, the core business of PayScale is to provide compensation data to corporate customers who use this data to determine wages for employees. In the past, PayScale was owned by Warburg Pincus, a private equity firm with a history of investing in for-profit colleges, including Bridgepoint Education. In 2014, Warburg Pincus announced its acquisition of PayScale for up to $100 million. For a discussion of Warburg Pincus's history of investing in for-profit colleges, see U.S. Senate Subcommittee on Health, Employment, Labor, and Pensions, *For Profit Higher Education: The Failure to Safeguard the Federal Investment and Ensure Student Success*, vol. 1 of 4 (Washington, DC: Government Printing Office, 2012), https://www.govinfo.gov /content/pkg/CPRT-112SPRT74931/pdf/CPRT-112SPRT74931.pdf (2012).

18. See "College Salary Report FAQs and Methodology," PayScale, 2017, https://web.archive.org/web/20180430010826/https://www.payscale.com /college-salary-report/methodology.

19. See "PayScale College Report FAQS," accessed April 15 2018, https:// www.payscale.com/college-roi/faqs.

20. See Doug Lederman, "PayScale's Impact (and Limitations)," *Inside Higher Ed*, April 18, 2017, https://www.insidehighered.com/news/2017/04/18/payscale -rankings-roi-have-influence-and-significant-limitations.

21. Joseph Altonji, Peter Arcidiacono, and Arnaud Maurel, "The Analysis of Field Choice in College and Graduate School: Determinants and Wage Effects," *Handbook of the Economics of Education* 5 (2016): tables 3 and 5.

22. See "PayScale College Report FAQs."

23. For a recent example, see American Academy of Arts and Sciences, *The State of the Humanities 2018: Graduates in the Workforce & Beyond* (Cambridge, MA: American Academy of Arts and Sciences, 2018).

24. Gallup and Purdue University, *Great Jobs, Great Lives: The 2014 Gallup-Purdue Index Report* (Washington, DC: Gallup, 2014), 15, https://www .gallup.com/services/176768/2014-gallup-purdue-index-report.aspx.

25. For spillover effects of higher education generally, see Enrico Moretti, "Estimating the Social Return to Higher Education: Evidence from Longitudinal and Repeated Cross-Sectional Data," *Journal of Econometrics* 121 (2004): 175–212; and Moretti, "Workers' Education, Spillovers, and Productivity: Evidence from Plant-Level Production Functions," *American Economic Review* 94, no. 3 (2004): 656–690. For effects on health, see Damon Clark and Heather Royer, "The Effect of Education on Adult Mortality and Health: Evidence from Britain," *American Economic Review* 103, no. 6 (2013): 2087–2120. For impact on civic engagement, see Thomas Dee, "Are There Civic Returns to Education?" *Journal of Public Economics* 88, nos. 9–10 (2004): 1697–1720. For impact on crime rates, see Lance Lochner and Enrico Moretti, "The Effect of Education on Crime: Evidence from Prison Inmates, Arrests, and Self-Reports," *American*

Economic Review 94, no. 1 (2004): 155–189. For a summary of the nonpecuniary and social returns to higher education, see Walter W. McMahon, *Higher Learning, Greater Good: The Private and Social Benefits of Higher Education* (Baltimore: Johns Hopkins University Press, 2009).

Chapter 2. University Rankings

1. Karen Durkin, "Gallaudet University Named No. 3 in the Nation for 'Best Value Schools' in U.S. News & World Report 2021 Best Colleges Rankings," PRWeb, September 14, 2020, accessed June 2021, https://www.prweb.com /releases/gallaudet_university_named_no_3_in_the_nation_for_best_value _schools_in_u_s_news_world_report_2021_best_colleges_rankings/prweb17390875 .htm#:~:text=Today%20Gallaudet%20University%20was%20recognized,the%20 same%20category%20l; Randon Coffey, "U.S. News & World Report Names Cottey College the Best in the Midwest Region," Cottey College, September 14, 2020, https://cottey.edu/2020/09/rankings/#:~:text=COVID%2D19-,U.S.%20NEWS%20 %26%20WORLD%20REPORT%20NAMES%20COTTEY%20COLLEGE,BEST%20 IN%20THE%20MIDWEST%20REGION&text=NEVADA%2C%20MO%E2%80%94 Today%2C%20U.S.,states%20comprising%20the%20Midwest%20region; Yasmin Anwar, "UC Berkeley Still No.1 Public, Fourth Best Globally in U.S. News Rankings," UC Berkeley, October 20, 2020, https://news.berkeley.edu/2020/10 /20/uc-berkeley-still-no-1-public-fourth-best-globally-in-u-s-news-rankings/.

2. Michael Luca and Jonathan Smith, "Salience in Quality Disclosure: Evidence from the U.S. News College Rankings," *Journal of Economics & Management Strategy* 22, no. 1 (2013): 58–77.

3. See Robert Morse and Eric Brooks, "A More Detailed Look at the Ranking Factors," *U.S. News*, September 12, 2021, https://www.usnews.com/education /best-colleges/articles/ranking-criteria-and-weights.

4. See the Jack Kent Cooke Foundation's list that classifies colleges and universities by selectivity at https://www.jkcf.org/wp-content/uploads/2018/06 /The_Transfer_Process-2015_list_of_selective_colleges.pdf.

5. Stacy Dale and Alan Krueger, "Estimating the Effects of College Characteristics over the Career Using Administrative Earnings Data," *Journal of Human Resources* 49, no. 2 (2014): 323–358.

6. Sarah R. Cohodes and Joshua S. Goodman, "Merit Aid, College Quality, and College Completion: Massachusetts' Adams Scholarship as an In-Kind Subsidy," *American Economic Journal: Applied Economics* 6, no. 4 (2014): 251–285.

7. Zachary Bleemer and Aashish Mehta, "College Major Restrictions and Student Stratification," Center for Studies in Higher Education Research and Occasional Papers 21, no. 14 (2021), https://cshe.berkeley.edu/publications/college -major-restrictions-and-student-stratification-zachary-bleemer-and-aashish-mehta.

8. Sandra E. Black, Jeffrey T. Denning, and Jesse Rothstein, "Winners and Losers? The Effect of Gaining and Losing Access to Selective Colleges on Educa-

tion and Labor Market Outcomes," National Bureau of Economic Research Working Paper 26821, March 2020, https://www.nber.org/system/files/working _papers/w26821/w26821.pdf; Zachary Bleemer, "Affirmative Action, Mismatch, and Economic Mobility after California's Proposition 209," *Quarterly Journal of Economics* 137, no. 1 (2022): 115–160.

9. Liz Foreman and Ashley Corinne Killough, "Freshmen Get $300 to Retake the SAT," *Baylor Lariat*, October 10, 2008, https://www.baylor.edu/content /services/document.php?id=73959.

10. Sara Rimer, "Baylor Rewards Freshmen Who Retake SAT," *New York Times*, October 14, 2008, https://www.nytimes.com/2008/10/15/education /15baylor.html.

11. Max Kutner, "How to Game the College Rankings," *Boston*, August 26, 2014, https://www.bostonmagazine.com/news/2014/08/26/how-northeastern -gamed-the-college-rankings.

12. Doug Lederman, "'Manipulating,' Er, Influencing 'U.S. News,'" *Inside Higher Ed*, June 3, 2009, https://www.insidehighered.com/news/2009/06/03 /manipulating-er-influencing-us-news.

13. For an in-depth discussion of gaming graduation rates, see Elizabeth A. Armstrong and Laura T. Hamilton, *Paying for the Party: How College Maintains Inequality* (Cambridge, MA: Harvard University Press, 2013).

Chapter 3. Selectivity

1. For example, Chetty and colleagues show that there is a great deal of variation across universities in their "value added," according to which better universities lead their students to much higher-paying careers than lower-quality universities. However, that paper does not illuminate which specific universities are "high quality." Raj Chetty, John N. Friedman, Emmanuel Saez, Nicholas Turner, and Danny Yagan, "Income Segregation and Intergenerational Mobility across Colleges in the United States," *Quarterly Journal of Economics* 135, no. 3: 1567–1633.

2. For admission rates for UC campuses, see University of California, University of California. "Undergraduate Admissions Summary," 2021, https:// www.universityofcalifornia.edu/about-us/information-center/admissions-residency -and-ethnicity.

3. Paul Tough, *The Years that Matter Most: How College Makes or Breaks Us* (Boston, MA: Houghton Mifflin Harcourt, 2019), 39.

4. Fung Bros., "UC Stereotypes Explained: UCLA, UCB, UCR, UCI etc.," YouTube video, September 11, 2014, https://www.youtube.com/watch?v=int3lFioTtU.

5. Harry Mok, "9 UC Campuses Ranked among World's Best Universities," University of California, August 15, 2014, https://www.universityofcalifornia.edu /news/9-uc-campuses-ranked-among-world%E2%80%99s-best-universities. See Niche's most recent ranking of the UC campuses at "University of California System," 2022, https://www.niche.com/colleges/university-of-california-system/.

Niche's somewhat ambiguous methodology is described at Niche, "The Best Colleges Methodology," https://about.niche.com/methodology/best-colleges/. For UC's recent rankings of its campuses, see "The 2017–2018 University of California Rankings Roundup," https://www.universityofcalifornia.edu/sites/default/files /2017-uc-rankings-chart.pdf.

6. Niche, "The Best Colleges Methodology." It's worth noting that Niche ranks UC Santa Cruz, UC Riverside, and UC Merced below the three most selective California State campuses (San Luis Obisbo, San Diego, and Long Beach), all of which are more selective than the three lower-ranked campuses.

7. Stacy Dale and Alan Krueger, "Estimating the Effects of College Characteristics over the Career Using Administrative Earnings Data," *Journal of Human Resources* 49, no. 2 (2014): 323.

8. For an example, see Brad J. Hershbein, "Worker Signals among New College Graduates: The Role of Selectivity and GPA," Upjohn Institute Working Papers 13, no. 190. January 1, 2013, https://research.upjohn.org/up_workingpapers/190/.

9. Quoted in in Valerie Strauss, "U.S. News Changed the Way It Ranks Colleges. It's Still Ridiculous," *Washington Post*, September 12, 2018, https:// www.washingtonpost.com/education/2018/09/12/us-news-changed-way-it-ranks -colleges-its-still-ridiculous/.

10. See, for example, Marta Bakula, "Record-Low Acceptance Rate as Applicant Numbers Increase," *Chicago Maroon*, April 14, 2015, https://www .chicagomaroon.com/2015/04/14/record-low-acceptance-rate-as-applicant -numbers-increase/.

11. Bakula, "Record-Low Acceptance Rate as Applicant Numbers Increase."

12. Eric Hoover, "Application Inflation: When Is Enough Enough?" *New York Times*, November 5, 2010, https://www.nytimes.com/2010/11/07/education /edlife/07HOOVER-t.html.

13. Hoover, "Application Inflation."

14. "University of Chicago," *U.S. News*, https://www.usnews.com/best -colleges/university-of-chicago-1774.

15. "*U.S. News* Rankings for 57 Leading Universities, 1983–2007," September 13, 2017, http://publicuniversityhonors.com/2017/09/13/u-s-news-rankings -for-57-leading-universities-1983-2007/. The University of Chicago also embarked on a large capital projects campaign, funded in part by the expansion of philanthropic gifts and of undergraduate enrollments and their tuition revenue.

16. For an example, see Michael Meranze and Christopher Newfield, "UCLA Loses Loni: Why Budget Silence Is Bad for Science," Remaking the University, May 12, 2013, http://utotherescue.blogspot.com/2013/05/ucla-loses-loni-why -budget-silence-is.html.

17. Jeff Levy, "The Great 'Success' of the University of Chicago," BigJ Educational Consulting, July 10, 2019, https://www.bigjeducationalconsulting .com/blog/finding-colleges-that-are-affordable.

18. National Center for Education Statistics, "Undergraduate Retention and Graduation Rates," fig. 4, last updated May 2022, https://nces.ed.gov/programs /coe/indicator/ctr.

19. Jolanta Juszkiewicz, *Trends in Community College Enrollment and Completion Data, 2016* (Washington, DC: American Association of Community Colleges, 2016), fig. 2. This report shows better outcomes over a longer period of time and for full-time students.

20. William G. Bowen, Matthew M. Chingos, and Michael S. McPherson, *Crossing the Finish Line: Completing College at America's Public Universities* (Princeton, NJ: Princeton University Press, 2009), 197.

21. Bowen, Chingos, and McPherson, *Crossing the Finish Line*, 198.

22. Bowen, Chingos, and McPherson say that they failed "to find an institutional resource effect" that would explain graduation rates. But that is because they didn't look for it: they claim a "lack of measures of resources that are truly comparable across universities"; *Crossing the Finish Line*, 200.

23. Bowen, Chingos, and McPherson, *Crossing the Finish Line*, 196.

24. For a valuable account of how such measures interact to help students at the University of Texas at Austin, see Paul Tough, "Who Gets to Graduate?" *New York Times*, May 15, 2014, http://www.nytimes.com/2014/05/18/magazine/who -gets-to-graduate.html.

25. More technically, they found a correlation between higher graduation rates and lower student net costs for the bottom half of the student body by income.

26. Sara Goldrick-Rab, *Paying the Price: College Costs, Financial Aid, and the Betrayal of the American Dream* (Chicago: University of Chicago Press, 2016).

27. This is true whether one uses complex definitions of educational quality based on cognitive gain and qualitative tests such as the Collegiate Learning Assessment or simpler, quantifiable measure such as graduation rates.

28. Richard Arum and Josipa Roksa, *Academically Adrift: Limited Learning on College Campuses* (Chicago: University of Chicago Press, 2011).

29. Donna M. Desrochers, Colleen M. Lenihan, and Jane V. Wellman, *Trends in College Spending, 1998–2008: Where Does the Money Come From? Where Does It Go? What Does It Buy?* (Washington, DC: Delta Cost Project, 2019), fig. 7.

30. Anthony P. Carnevale and Jeff Strohl, *Separate & Unequal* (Washington, DC: Georgetown University Center on Education and the Workforce, 2013), 7, https://1gyhoq479ufd3yna29x7ubjn-wpengine.netdna-ssl.com/wp-content /uploads/SeparateUnequal.ES_.pdf.

31. Zach Bleemer conducted this analysis. He chose two outcome variables— four- and six-year graduation rates—and estimated regressions on three samples: all American universities in the Integrated Postsecondary Education System (about 1,500, although only 1,200 report student SAT statistics), the top 100 public universities, and the top 200 nonprofit private universities. (In the overall group there are about twice as many private as public universities. The study excluded

for-profit universities and two-year institutions.) Bleemer ranked universities by the 75th percentile of SAT math scores of their student bodies: schools made the cut with a 630 (public) or 620 (private) score. He estimated two linear regression models: How do selectivity levels compare to per-student expenditures in predicting graduation rates by themselves? And how do they compare when they are mixed in with other university-specific indicators that an applicant could know, such as the average SAT scores of a school or whether it's private or which state it is in (and what universities in that state are like)? The analysis of the data here shows the importance of selectivity and instructional spending for increasing an understanding of graduation rates *on top of what a person already knows*.

32. Christopher Newfield, *The Great Mistake: How We Wrecked Public Universities and How We Can Fix Them* (Baltimore: Johns Hopkins University Press, 2016), 271. For technical reasons related to UC's disclosures, the difference in spending between the two institutions may be far higher.

33. National Center for Education Statistics, "Postsecondary Institution Expenses," last updated May 2021, https://nces.ed.gov/programs/coe/indicator /cue.

34. See, for example, Mary Helen Immordino-Yang, "Studying the Effects of Culture by Integrating Neuroscientific With Ethnographic Approaches," *Psychological Inquiry* 24, no. 1 (2013): 42–46, https://doi.org/10.1080/1047840X.2013 .770278.

35. As of May 2022, the data could be downloaded at U.S. Department of Education College Scorecard (https://collegescorecard.ed.gov/). Astonishingly, per-student instructional expenditure is the 383rd column of the full dataset with the data label "INEXPFTE."

36. David Deming and Christopher Walters present compelling evidence that increased student expenditure translates into improved student outcomes such as the likelihood of degree attainment; see "The Impact of Price Caps and Spending Cuts on U.S. Postsecondary Attainment," National Bureau of Economic Research Working Papers 23736, August 2017, https://www.nber.org/papers/w23736.

37. "Someone once asked Slick Willie Sutton, the bank robber, why he robbed banks. The question might have uncovered a tale of injustice and lifelong revenge. Maybe a banker foreclosed on the old homestead, maybe a banker's daughter spurned Sutton for another. Sutton looked a little surprised, as if he had been asked 'Why does a smoker light a cigarette?' 'I rob banks because that's where the money is,' he said." Robert M. Yoder, "Someday They'll Get Slick Willie Sutton," *Saturday Evening Post*, January 20, 1951, 17.

Chapter 4. Tuition Sticker Price

1. For historical Columbia undergraduate population, see Bureau of Education, *Biennial Survey of Education: 1920–1922* (Washington, DC: Government Printing Office, 1925); and William W. Ferrier, *Origin and Development of*

the University of California (Berkeley, CA: The Sather Gate Book Shop, 1930). For recent data on Columbia's graduation rates, see "Columbia University Facts 2016," https://opir.columbia.edu/sites/default/files/content/Columbia%20Facts/Facts _2016.pdf. See "Columbia University Facts 2017" for number of applications; https://opir.columbia.edu/sites/default/files/content/Columbia%20Facts/Facts _2017.pdf. The US population is from United States Census Bureau, "Historical Population Change Data (1910–2020)," April 26, 2021, https://www.census.gov /data/tables/time-series/dec/popchange-data-text.html. The college-going population is from Claudia Goldin Lawrence F. Katz, and Ilyana Kuziemko, "The Homecoming of American College Women: The Reversal of the College Gender Gap," *Journal of Economic Perspectives* 20, no. 4 (2006): 133–156. Columbia statistics include the School of General Studies, which didn't exist in the 1920s; if the School of General Studies is excluded from the data, Columbia has grown by only 22% since 1921.

2. Statistics from Raj Chetty, John N. Friedman, Emmanuel Saez, Nicholas Turner, and Danny Yagan, "Mobility Report Cards: The Role of Colleges in Intergenerational Mobility," National Bureau of Economic Research Working Papers 23618, July 2017, https://www.nber.org/papers/w23618. See also "Economic Diversity and Student Outcomes at America's Colleges and Universities: Find Your College," The Upshot, n.d. [2017], https://www.nytimes.com /interactive/projects/college-mobility.

3. Interestingly, Columbia is actually the most financially representative university in the Ivy League; it has lower median incomes and more bottom-quintile students than any other such school. Princeton, for example, pulls 72% of its students from the top income quintile, and only 2.1% of Yale's students are from the bottom income quintile. Students at Brown and Dartmouth have median family incomes over $200,000. See "Economic Diversity and Student Outcomes at America's Colleges and Universities."

4. Columbia University, Financial Aid & Educational Financing, "Facts and Figures: 2022–2023 Costs," https://cc-seas.financialaid.columbia.edu/eligibility /facts.

5. In fact, according to May 2022 data at the U.S. Department of Education's College Scorecard, at least 8% of Columbia students receive federal loans and the average debt among graduate borrowers is $21,500. U.S. Department of Education College Scorecard, "Columbia University in the City of New York," last updated May 2, 2022, https://collegescorecard.ed.gov/school/?190150 -Columbia-University-in-the-City-of-New-York. As recently as 2018, the College Scorecard reported that 26% of Columbia students received federal loans.

6. U.S. Department of Education College Scorecard, "Columbia University in the City of New York."

7. U.S. Department of Education College Scorecards: "SUNY at Albany," last updated June 15, 2022, https://collegescorecard.ed.gov/school/?196060-SUNY

-at-Albany; "Pace University," last updated June 15, 2022, https://collegescore card.ed.gov/school/?194310-Pace-University.

8. This was true when we accessed the *U.S. News* website in 2018 and 2021.

9. World University Rankings, "Wall Street Journal/Times Higher Education College Rankings 2018," https://www.timeshighereducation.com/rankings/united -states/2018#!/page/0/length/25/sort_by/rank/sort_order/asc/cols/stats; Christian Kreznar, ed., "America's Top Colleges: The First Time a Public School Is Number One," 2022, https://www.forbes.com/top-colleges/.

10. The survey was conducted by the Federal Reserve Bank of New York as part of their monthly Survey of Consumer Expectations. The 1,150 randomly selected and nationally representative respondents, each of whom was a self-described "household head," were paid $15 for their participation. See Zachary Bleemer and Basit Zafar, "Intended College Attendance: Evidence from an Experiment on College Returns and Costs," *Journal of Public Economics* 157 (2018): 184–211.

11. Data presented in Sandy Baum and Jennifer Ma, *Trends in College Pricing, 2013* (New York: The College Board, 2013), which uses data collected from College Board's Annual Survey of Colleges.

12. We assumed that the small number of respondents who reported expected annual costs above $80,000 misread the question and instead had reported their expected cost of attending a university for four years. We divided those responses by 4. We then winsorized the data, replacing the bottom 5% of respondents with the 5th percentile estimate and the top 5% of respondents with the 95th percentile estimate in order to remove outliers. Median responses tended to be slightly lower than the mean responses reported here.

13. Overall net prices at public and private universities rose in this period as a result of increasing housing costs. We used estimates of net tuition and fees from College Board, *Trends in College Pricing and Student Aid 2020* (New York: College Board, 2020).

14. Caroline Hoxby and Christopher Avery, "The Missing 'One-Offs': The Hidden Supply of High-Achieving, Low-Income Students," Brookings Papers on Economic Activity 2013, no. 1 (2013): 1–65.

15. See, e.g., David Deming and Christopher Walters, "The Impact of Price Caps and Spending Cuts on U.S. Postsecondary Attainment," National Bureau of Economic Research Working Papers 23736, August 2017, https://www.nber.org /papers/w23736.

16. As our book neared publication, a new study provided additional evidence that sticker prices dissuade high-achieving students from enrolling at public flagship universities even when the sticker price increases do not mean higher average net prices for students. See Phillip B. Levine, Jennifer Ma, and Lauren C. Russell, "Do College Applicants Respond to Changes in Sticker Prices Even When They Don't Matter?" National Bureau of Economic Research Working Papers 26910, March 2020, https://www.nber.org/papers/w26910.

17. Caroline Hoxby and Sarah Turner, "Expanding College Opportunities for High-Achieving, Low Income Students," Stanford Institute for Economic Policy Research Discussion Papers 12, no. 14, March 2013, https://siepr.stanford.edu/publications/working-paper/expanding-college-opportunities-high-achieving-low-income-students.

18. Oded Gurantz, Jessica Howell, Michael Hurwitz, Cassandra Larson, Matea Pender, and Brooke White, "A National-Level Information Experiment to Promote Enrollment in Selective Universities," *Journal of Policy Analysis and Management* 40, no. 2 (2021): 453–479.

19. See Carol Fuller and Carlo Salerno, *Information Required to Be Disclosed Under the Higher Education Act of 1965: Suggestions for Dissemination (Updated)* (Washington, DC: National Postsecondary Education Collective, 2009). The mandate is from Section 111 of the Higher Education Opportunity Act. You can also find a financial aid calculator at U.S. Department of Education, "Net Price Calculator," https://nces.ed.gov/ipeds/netpricecalculator/.

20. See three articles by David Leonhardt: "Getting a Clearer Picture of College Costs," Economix, September 18, 2013, https://economix.blogs.nytimes.com/2013/09/18/getting-a-clearer-picture-of-college-costs/; "A Simpler Financial-Aid Calculator Spreads," New York Times, September 21, 2015, https://www.nytimes.com/2015/09/22/upshot/a-simpler-financial-aid-calculator-spreads.html; and "Top Colleges Are Cheaper than You Think (Unless You're Rich)," *New York Times*, June 5, 2018, https://www.nytimes.com/interactive/2018/06/05/opinion/columnists/what-college-really-costs.html.

21. Phillip B. Levine, "Transparency in College Costs," Economic Studies Working Paper, November 2014, Brookings Institution, Washington, DC.

22. U.S. Department of Education College Scorecard, "Find the Right Fit," updated May 2, 2022, https://collegescorecard.ed.gov/.

23. Susan Dynarski C. J. Libassi, Katherine Michelmore, and Stephanie Owen, "Closing the Gap: The Effect of Reducing Complexity and Uncertainty in College Pricing on the Choices of Low-Income Students," *American Economic Review* 111, no. 6 (2021): 1721–1756.

24. See Urban Institute, "Understanding College Affordability: How Students, Institutions, and the Public Pay for Higher Education," 2017, http://collegeaffordability.urban.org/.

Chapter 5. Scorekeeping Student Debt

1. Center for Microeconomic Data, *Quarterly Report on Household Debt and Credit: 2021 Q1* (New York: New York Federal Reserve Bank, 2021), https://www.newyorkfed.org/medialibrary/interactives/householdcredit/data/pdf/HHDC_2021Q1.pdf.

2. For a thorough overview of the problem in the United States, including a detailed discussion of how it has evolved in the context of the California university

system, see Christopher Newfield, *The Great Mistake: How We Wrecked Public Universities and How We Can Fix Them* (Baltimore: Johns Hopkins University Press, 2016), 190–222; Bob Meister, "Debt and Taxes: Can the Financial Industry Save Public Universities?" *Representations* 116, no. 1 (2011): 128–155; Zachary Bleemer, Meta Brown, Donghoon Lee, Katherine Strair, and Wilbert van der Klaauw, "Echoes of Rising Tuition in Students' Borrowing, Educational Attainment, and Homeownership in Post-Recession America," *Journal of Urban Economics* 122 (2021): 103298; and Zachary Bleemer, Meta Brown, Donghoon Lee, and Wilbert van der Klaauw, "Tuition, Jobs, or Housing: What's Keeping Millennials at Home?" *Federal Reserve Bank of New York Staff Reports* 700, November 2014. In her analysis of an anti-debt student protest in California and the crisis conditions related to that social movement, Amy McClanahan also provides a broad overview of the problem, including the way widespread student debt has opened up a new front of social struggle; see "The Living Indebted: Student Militancy and the Financialization of Debt," *Qui Parle* 20, no. 1 (2011): 57–77. For historical overviews of the development of federal student loan systems in the United States, see Joel Best and Eric Best, *The Student Loan Mess: How Good Intentions Created a Trillion-Dollar Problem* (Berkeley: University of California Press, 2014); Elizabeth Popp Berman and Abby Stivers, "Student Loans as a Pressure on U.S. Higher Education," in *The University under Pressure*, ed. Elizabeth Popp Berman and Catherine Paradeise (Bingley, UK: Emerald Publishing, 2016), 132–143; and Enyu Zhou and Pilar Mendoza, "Financing Higher Education in the United States: A Historical Overview of Loans in Federal Financial Aid Policy," in *The Neoliberal Agenda and the Student Debt Crisis in U.S. Higher Education*, ed. Nicholas D. Hartlep, Lucille L. T. Eckrich, and Brandon O. Hensley (New York: Routledge, 2017). For a look at the development of the high-tuition, high-debt system in the UK, see Andrew McGettigan, *The Great University Gamble* (London: Pluto Press, 2013), 25–51.

  3. Strike Debt!'s motto, "You are not a loan," nicely captures their movement against debt subjectivity, or in other words, against allowing people to be defined by their financial debts. Their broader ambition is for a widespread jubilee, a nineteenth-century word referring to a recurrent celebration of widespread emancipation from slavery. In what Strike Debt calls a "rolling jubilee," it uses donations to buy up and cancel devalued debt (in default). See Strike Debt, *The Debt Resisters' Operations Manual* (Oakland, CA: PM Press, 2014), https://strikedebt .org/drom/#toc, especially chapter 4, "Student Debt: Foreclosing on the Future" (https://strikedebt.org/drom/#toc).

  4. There is a similar movement on the political left in the UK, where the Labour Party has pledged to abolish tuition fees and, presumably, forgive some if not all student loans that have existed to a significant degree since 2010.

  5. Caitlin Zaloom, *Indebted: How Families Make College Work at Any Cost* (Princeton, NJ: Princeton University Press, 2019).

  6. Zaloom, *Indebted*.

7. In the economics literature, these are usually referred to as income contingent loans. After making regular payments for 20 to 30 years, remaining balances are forgiven. As such, these loans are actually a hybrid between a loan and a tax, as the amount of principle and the length of the "contract" changes based on the income of the borrower; see Gareth Bryant and Ben Spies-Butcher, "Bringing Finance Inside the State: How Income-Contingent Loans Blur the Boundaries between Debt and Tax," *Environment and Planning A: Economy & Space* 52, no. 1 (2020): 111–129. In the United States, these are called income driven repayment (IDR) plans, and the Department of Education offers four types. The U.S. Consumer Financial Protection Bureau provides a useful overview of US IDR plans in Thomas Conklin and Christa Gibbs, *Data Point: Borrower Experiences on Income-Driven Repayment* (Washington, DC: Consumer Financial Protection Bureau, 2019) https://files.consumerfinance.gov/f/documents/cfpb_data-point_borrower -experiences-on-IDR.pdf. For all of these plans, monthly payments are capped at between 10 and 20% of discretionary income. The complicated equation that determines discretionary income and other useful information can be found at "Discretionary Income," Federal Aid, U.S. Department of Education, https:// studentaid.gov/help-center/answers/topic/glossary/article/discretionary-income. Additional useful information on IDR eligibility can be found in the U.S. Department of Education, Office of Inspector General, "The Department's Communication Regarding the Costs of Income-Driven Repayment Plans and Loan Forgiveness Programs," January 31, 2018, https://www2.ed.gov/about/offices/list/oig /auditreports/fy2018/a09q0003.pdf.

While the data are imperfect, as of 2019 the Department of Education estimates that 30% of indebted former students have applied to and been enrolled in one of these plans. Eligibility for each is dependent on a series of criteria that includes when the loans were initiated, marital status and number of dependents, and level of income. Unlike standard repayment plans, which are more like a standard mortgage and last for ten years, IDRs last between 20 and 25 years and are typically better suited to those with lower incomes or those who have experienced some kind of financial turmoil, including unemployment.

8. Berman and Stivers, "Student Loans as a Pressure on U.S. Higher Education."

9. This system of accountability begins when students fill out the Department of Education Free Application for Student Aid (FAFSA) form, which forces students, and more often their parents to provide wide ranging and detailed financial information.

10. Michael Sandel, *What Money Can't Buy: The Moral Limits of Markets* (New York: Farrar, Straus and Giroux, 2012).

11. David O. Lucca, Taylor Nadauld, and Karen Shen, "Credit Supply and the Rise in College Tuition: Evidence from the Expansion in Federal Student Aid Programs," *Review of Financial Studies* 32, no. 2 (2019): 423–466; Newfield, *The*

Great Mistake; Meister, "Debt and Taxes"; Charlie Eaton, "Still Public: State Universities and America's New Student-Debt Coalitions," *PS: Political Science & Politics* 50, no. 2 (2017): 408–412.

12. The first year that US federal loans outpaced federal grants was 1981; Zhou and Mendoza, "Financing Higher Education in the United States," 11.

13. Quoted in Best and Best, *The Student Loan Mess*, 31.

14. Best and Best, *The Student Loan Mess*, 66.

15. Zaloom, *Indebted*, 14.

16. Bethany McLean, "Sallie Mae: A Hot Stock, a Tough Lender," *CNN Money*, December 14, 2005, https://money.cnn.com/2005/12/14/news /fortune500/sallie_fortune_122605/index.htm.

17. James B. Steele and Lance Williams, "Who Got Rich Off the Student Debt Crisis?" *Reveal*, June 28, 2016, https://revealnews.org/article/who-got-rich -off-the-student-debt-crisis/.

18. Best and Best, *The Student Loan Mess*, 47.

19. See Meister, "Debt and Taxes."

20. See Best and Best, *The Student Loan Mess*, 43–75.

21. Charles A. Jeszeck, "Older Americans: Inability to Repay Student Loans May Affect Financial Security of a Small Percentage of Retirees," testimony before the Special Committee on Aging, U.S. Senate (Washington, DC: GAO, 2014), 17, https://www.gao.gov/assets/gao-14-866t.pdf.

22. In the speech where he launched the initiative that would become the College Scorecard, Obama said, "A higher education is the single best investment you can make in your future. And I'm proud of all the students who are making that investment. And that's not just me saying it. Look, right now, the unemployment rate for Americans with at least a college degree is about one-third lower than the national average. The incomes of folks who have at least a college degree are more than twice those of Americans without a high school diploma. So more than ever before, some form of higher education is the surest path into the middle class"; Barack Obama, "Remarks by the President on College Affordability—Buffalo, NY," August 23, 2013, https://obamawhitehouse .archives.gov/the-press-office/2013/08/22/remarks-president-college-affordability -buffalo-ny.

23. U.S. Department of Education Press Office, "Secretary DeVos Delivers on Promise to Provide Students Relevant, Actionable Information Needed to Make Personalized Education Decisions," U.S. Department of Education Press Office, November 20, 2019, https://content.govdelivery.com/accounts/USED/bulletins /26d1286.

24. Wendy Brown, *Undoing the Demos: Neoliberalism's Stealth Revolution* (New York: Zone Books, 2015).

25. Brown focuses on the decline of the liberal arts at public universities and its effects on democratic institutions in *Undoing the Demos*, 175–200. Eric

Alterman focuses specifically on the decline of history majors at public universities, which has obvious links to students' concerns about future wages in "The Decline of Historical Thinking," *New Yorker*, February 4, 2019, https://www.newyorker.com/news/news-desk/the-decline-of-historical -thinking. Not surprisingly, student enrollment in computer science majors, where early-career future wages tend to be much higher, has accelerated at public universities.

26. David Graeber, *Debt: The First 5,000 Years* (Brooklyn, NY: Melville House, 2011), 14.

27. Zaloom, *Indebted*.

28. Alexander Bartik and Scott T. Nelson, "Credit Reports as Resumes: The Incidence of Pre-Employment Credit Screening," *MIT Department of Economics Graduate Student Research Papers* 16, no. 01, March 7, 2016.

29. McClanahan, "The Living Indebted"; McClanahan, *Dead Pledges: Debt, Crisis, and Twenty-First-Century Culture* (Stanford, CA: Stanford University Press, 2017).

30. McClanahan, "The Living Indebted."

31. Newfield, *The Great Mistake*; Meister, "Debt and Taxes"; Brown, *Undoing the Demos*.

Chapter 6. Average Wages by College Major

1. Anthony P. Carnevale, Ban Cheah, and Andrew R. Hanson, *The Economic Value of College Majors* (Washington, DC: Georgetown University Center on Education and the Workforce, 2015).

2. Center on Education and the Workforce, "The Economic Value of College Majors," 2015, https://cew.georgetown.edu/cew-reports/valueofcollegemajors/.

3. Quoted in Patricia Cohen, "A Rising Call to Promote STEM Education and Cut Liberal Arts Funding," *New York Times*, February 21, 2016, https://www .nytimes.com/2016/02/22/business/a-rising-call-to-promote-stem-education-and -cut-liberal-arts-funding.html.

4. See "UC Alumni at Work," University of California, https://www .universityofcalifornia.edu/infocenter/uc-alumni-work; and "Seek UT," University of Texas, http://seekut.utsystem.edu/.

5. See Amber Bloomfield, "College Measures," n.d., American Institutes for Research, accessed May 2018, https://www.air.org/center/college-measures/.

6. American Institutes for Research, "In Minnesota, Majors Matter, AIR Study Finds; Future Earnings Linked to College Course of Study," AIR, October 4, 2016, accessed May 2018, https://www.air.org/news/press-release/minnesota-majors -matter-air-study-finds-future-earnings-linked-college-course.

7. See "Mark Schneider, Director, Institute of Education Science— Biography," U.S. Department of Education, last modified May 10, 2018, https:// www2.ed.gov/news/staff/bios/schneider.html.

8. Matthew Wiswall and Basit Zafar, "Determinants of College Major Choice: Identification using an Information Experiment," *Review of Economic Studies* 82, no. 2 (2015): 791–824.

9. Wiswall and Zafar, "Determinants of College Major Choice," 821.

10. Peter Arcidiacono, "Ability Sorting and the Returns to College Major," *Journal of Econometrics* 121, nos. 1–2 (2004): 343–375, calculations from table 12.

11. See Ralph Stinebrickner and Todd R. Stinebrickner, "A Major in Science? Initial Beliefs and Final Outcomes for College Major and Dropout," *Review of Economic Studies* 81, no. 1 (2014): 426–472.

12. Arcidiacono, "Ability Sorting and the Returns to College Major," calculations from table 12.

13. Matthew Wiswall and Basit Zafar, "Preference for the Workplace, Human Capital, and Gender," National Bureau of Economic Research Working Papers 22173, April 2016, https://www.nber.org/papers/w22173.

14. Statistics calculated from the 2019 American Community Survey; Steven Ruggles, Sarah Flood, Ronald Goeken, Josiah Grover, Erin Meyer, Jose Pacas, and Matthew Sobek, "U.S. Census Data for Social, Economic, and Health Research," 2020, https://usa.ipums.org/usa/. Managerial occupations include 2018 American Community Survey occupation scores 10–440. Arts and humanities include area studies, English, history, philosophy, foreign languages, and theology.

15. See Abby Jackson, "The 3 Most Popular Majors at Every Ivy League School," Insider, February 16, 2018, https://www.businessinsider.com/most -popular-ivy-league-major-2017-4.

16. Carnevale, Cheah, and Hanson, *The Economic Value of College Majors*.

17. Arcidiacono, "Ability Sorting and the Returns to College Major."

18. See the FAQ tab of "UC Alumni at Work" (https://www.universityof california.edu/infocenter/uc-alumni-work).

19. Consider, for example, a violinist who is employed by an orchestra eight months a year but is laid off for the summer months. Depending on how the violinist's employment fell across the year's quarters, the university would likely assume that the missing quarter of wages were an anomaly and "fill them in" with a regular quarter's wages, making it appear that the violinist's wages were higher than they were.

20. Stinebrickner and Stinebrickner, "A Major in Science?"

21. Highest unemployment rate from Table A-4 of Zachary Bleemer, "Top Percent Policies and the Return to Postsecondary Selectivity," Center for Studies in Higher Education Research and Occasional Papers 21, no. 1, January 2021, https://cshe.berkeley.edu/publications/top-percent-policies-and-return -postsecondary-selectivity-zachary-bleemer-cshe-121.

22. See Rebecca Diamond and Enrico Moretti, "Where Is Standard of Living the Highest? Local Prices and the Geography of Consumption," National Bureau of

Economic Research Working Papers 29533, December 2021, https://www.nber
.org/papers/w29533.

23. Statistics from Zachary Bleemer and Yuri Jeon's analysis of American
Community Survey data (Ruggles et al., "U.S. Census Data for Social, Economic,
and Health Research").

24. See MN Office of Higher Education, "Graduates Earnings by Program &
Institution," accessed May 2018, https://web.archive.org/web/20180926125143
/http://www.mnedtrends.org/Report/compare-graduate-earnings-programs-and
-institutions.

25. Raj Chetty, John N. Friedman, Emmanuel Saez, Nicholas Turner, and
Danny Yagan, "Mobility Report Cards: The Role of Colleges in Intergenerational
Mobility," 17–18 and fig. II, National Bureau of Economic Research Working
Papers 23618, July 2017, https://www.nber.org/papers/w23618.

26. See Zachary Bleemer, "The UC ClioMetric History Project and Formatted
Optical Character Recognition," Center for Studies in Higher Education Research
and Occasional Papers 18, no. 3, 2018, https://cshe.berkeley.edu/publications/uc
-cliometric-history-project-and-formatted-optical-character-recognition-zachary;
and University of California, "Long-Run Outcomes for UC Berkeley Alumni,"
https://www.universityofcalifornia.edu/infocenter/berkeley-outcomes.

27. Lars J. Kirkeboen, Edwin Leuven, and Magne Mogstad, "Field of Study,
Earnings, and Self-Selection," *Quarterly Journal of Economics* 131, no. 3 (2016):
1057–1111.

28. A recent study written by two of our coauthors shows that students who
prefer to pursue economics receive a large wage return from being allowed into
that major at UC Santa Cruz. This could provide useful information to students
considering that major, although there is a surprising dearth of dependable
information about other specific fields of study. Zachary Bleemer and Aashish
Mehta, "Will Studying Economics Make You Rich? A Regression Discontinuity
Analysis of the Returns to College Major," *American Economic Journal: Applied
Economics* 14, no. 2 (2022): 1–22.

29. Wiswall and Zafar, "Determinants of College Major Choice."

30. National Academy of Sciences, National Academy of Engineering, and
Institute of Medicine, *Rising above the Gathering Storm* (Washington, DC: National
Academies Press, 2007); National Academy of Sciences, National Academy of
Engineering, and Institute of Medicine, *Rising above the Gathering Storm, Revisited*
(Washington, DC: National Academies Press, 2010).

Chapter 7. Access to Your Preferred Major

1. We focus in this chapter on the unintended consequences of restricting
entry into majors. However, it is worth noting, particularly for university faculty
and administrators, that these restrictions do not, as is sometimes argued, help
students find their strengths. Flunking out of freshman chemistry and ending up

with a history major tells a student (at best) that they began college lacking some skills that aspiring chemists can pick up during high school and college and that history is open to all comers. It will not tell them whether their interests and aptitudes will make them better at chemistry or history by the time they graduate.

2. For a flavor of the intended public commitment to equitable educational opportunity, see the 1960 California Master Plan for Higher Education (https:// regents.universityofcalifornia.edu/regmeet/july02/302attach1.pdf), which prescribed distinctive roles for the University of California, Cal State, and California community college systems with the explicit goal of ensuring broad access. The 1965 federal Higher Education Act introduced Pell Grants for the same reason.

3. See, e.g., Yossi Shavit, Richard Arum, and Adam Gamoran, *Stratification in Higher Education: A Comparative Study* (Stanford, CA: Stanford University Press, 2017); and Paul Tough, *The Years that Matter Most: How College Makes or Breaks Us* (Boston, MA: Houghton Mifflin Harcourt, 2019).

4. See Zachary Bleemer and Aashish Mehta, "College Major Restrictions and Student Stratification," Center for Studies in Higher Education Research and Occasional Papers 21, no. 14, 2021, https://cshe.berkeley.edu/publications /college-major-restrictions-and-student-stratification-zachary-bleemer-and-aashish -mehta.

5. Students whose families earn less than $50,000 per year are eligible for Federal Pell Grants.

6. A rather different critique of the *U.S. News* "Top Performers on Social Mobility" list could be made that exemplifies the point that some metrics do not reveal behavior so much as shape it. These rankings reward universities richly for admitting students below the $50,000 threshold but not for admitting those above it. Work by Caroline Hoxby and Christopher Avery showed that Pell grants were not helping their recipients enough, in part because elite colleges let in very few Pell Grant recipients; see "The Missing 'One-Offs': The Hidden Supply of High-Achieving, Low-Income Students," Brookings Papers on Economic Activity 2013, no. 1 (2013): 1–65. This focused public attention on admissions rates of Pell Grant recipients. A paper by Caroline Hoxby and Sarah Turner shows that, presumably in response, universities have begun admitting more students with incomes just low enough to qualify for Pell Grants but have cut back admissions among low-income students above the Pell Grant threshold even more; see "Measuring Opportunity in Higher Education," National Bureau of Economic Research Working Papers 25479, January 2019, https://www.nber.org/system /files/working_papers/w25479/w25479.pdf. The *U.S. News* social mobility rankings appear to reward similar behavior.

7. For example, according to UCSB's Net Price Calculator (https://www .finaid.ucsb.edu/net-price-calculator, accessed in July 2019), a child of a single parent earning $60,000 per year who has $30,000 in assets and two children in

college can expect to annually take on $5,500 in direct unsubsidized loans from the federal government. That student's parent can borrow an additional $4,352 if they pass a required credit check and the student can work to earn $3,000 in a work-study program. The interest on both loans will begin to accumulate within 60 days after they first borrow, adding to incentives for the student to work part time while in school. These calculations also assume that room and board costs less than $12,000 per year (a figure that is plausible only if one assumes that the student will rent half of a room in a shared house and almost never eat out) and exclude additional costs related to study-abroad programs, which the university strongly encourages.

8. Many of these decisions and behaviors show up in the university's biannual Undergraduate Education Survey. For example, in 2018, UCSB's Pell Grant recipients were 40% more likely to have started working a part-time job while in school than students who were not Pell recipients, and those who worked before college were 53% more likely to have increased their work hours after starting college. It is easy to see why: 61% of Pell-Grant recipients reported experiencing food insecurity and 9% reported experiencing homelessness, compared with 37% and 6%, respectively, among those not on Pell Grants. The survey considers a respondent to be food insecure if they responded affirmatively to either "I was worried whether my food would run out before I got more" or "The food that I bought just didn't last, and I didn't have money to get more." Homelessness means not having stable or reliable housing at any point during the school year. For details, see University of California, "Student Basic Needs," https://www.universityofcalifornia.edu/infocenter/student-basic-needs.

9. The undergraduate headcount, which started at 17,200 in 1999, grew by only about 1,000 in the decade leading up to the 2008 financial crisis. The increase over the decade after the crisis was almost four times as large.

10. A family income of $80,000 per year is the threshold to qualify for UC's Blue and Gold Opportunity Plan. The share of families below this threshold, which had fallen to 38% on the eve of the 2008 financial crisis, increased to 48% by 2016.

11. Our calculations, based on institutional data released by UCSB, show that real per-student expenditures increased gradually, from $25,300 in 2003 to $29,200 in 2016. However, state funding decreased from $15,200 per student in 2003 to $8,000 in 2011, then made a partial recovery to $11,100 in 2016. To make up for this lost state funding, average per-student tuition revenue grew from $10,100 in 2003 to $18,100 in 2016. Financial aid formulas were tweaked to protect lower-income students from the rising tuition load, and the best available data suggest these efforts were mostly successful. According to data from the Integrated Postsecondary Education Data System, the net cost of attending UCSB for a Title IV first-year student whose family income was between $30,000 and $48,000 per year rose from $10,400 in 2008–2009 to $11,500 in 2017–2018, adjusted for inflation.

12. To properly reflect student experience, we weighted each class by the number of students in it. For example, suppose that a university teaches 50 classes at 20 students per class and 50 classes at 100 students per class. By simply averaging the class size across classes, as might seem natural, one might conclude that the average class size is 60 ($50\% \times 20 + 50\% \times 100$). This is misleading. Only 1,000 seats are available in 20-person courses, but 5,000 seats are available in 100-person classes, so roughly 5 out of every 6 classes a student takes will be a 100-person class. We therefore calculate that the typical student at this university would experience an average class size of 86.23 ($\frac{1}{6} \times 20 + \frac{5}{6} \times 100$). Statistics on class size are not always calculated in this way. Data from Zachary Bleemer, "The UC ClioMetric History Project and Formatted Optical Character Recognition," Center for Studies in Higher Education Research and Occasional Papers 18, no. 3, 2018, https://cshe.berkeley.edu/publications/uc-cliometric-history-project-and -formatted-optical-character-recognition-zachary.

13. Another way to look at this is to see how far class sizes are from a pedagogical gold standard. We have compared data on class sizes to comparable courses at Stanford University in 2018–2019. In 2000, class sizes for UCSB students were, on average, 47% larger than comparable courses at Stanford University in 2018–2019. By 2016, they were 71% larger.

14. It is difficult to increase the number of seats in a course because many faculty refuse to dilute the quality of their remaining small classes by making them bigger and because the classrooms needed to make large classes bigger are already completely booked during the times that students and faculty are available to be in class. Several interdisciplinary minors actually became impossible to complete because of restrictions on course entry and had to be shelved.

15. Tyler Hayden, "UCSB Course Shortage at 'Crisis' Level, Dean Says," *Santa Barbara Independent*, September 15, 2021, https://www.independent.com /2021/09/15/ucsb-course-shortage-at-crisis-level-dean-says/.

16. *U.S. News* does not explain why particular colleges have moved up and down in their rankings. Moreover, the rankings are not intended to be compared over time. However, UCSB faculty are making excellent research contributions by any standard, which improves UCSB's reputation. *U.S. News* weights an institution's reputation heavily.

17. National Academy of Sciences, National Academy of Engineering, and Institute of Medicine, *Rising above the Gathering Storm* (Washington, DC: National Academies Press, 2007); National Academy of Sciences, National Academy of Engineering, and Institute of Medicine, *Rising above the Gathering Storm, Revisited* (Washington, DC: National Academies Press, 2010).

18. Unless otherwise specified, the statistics in the remainder of this chapter combine data from the UC Cliometric project with data from the UCSB Planning and Databooks. We downloaded the latter in 2019, but they have since been taken offline.

19. These wage-by-major estimates are recent national averages and do not change over time. A larger gap implies that the majors that URMs tend to complete majors with higher average earnings than the majors that non-URMs tend to complete.

20. To produce Figure 7.2 and this analysis of predicted employment rates, we used data from the latest American Community Survey to estimate the mean national earnings and mean national employment rate among recent college graduates with a major. We then weighted each major in each year by the percentage of URMs and non-URMs that completed them and reported the average of the two mean employment outcomes across the majors typically completed by each of the groups. These average outcomes thus differ for URM and non-URM graduates only because these two groups have different propensities to complete high-wage and low-wage majors.

21. Philip Babcock tested this idea carefully. He analyzed student-reported data from 338,414 course evaluations for 6,753 courses taught by 1,568 UC San Diego instructors. His main conclusion is that students' "average study time would be about 50% lower in a class in which the average expected grade was an A than in the same course taught by the same instructor in which students expected a C." He notes that these are likely underestimates because to the extent that causality is reversed, more effort should be associated with higher grades. More revealing still, he shows that students study less if other students in the same class expect higher grades. This suggests that they are not simply studying less because they are confident in their own ability to score well. See Babcock, "Real Costs of Nominal Grade Inflation? New Evidence from Student Course Evaluations," *Economic Inquiry* 48, no. 4 (2010): 983–996. Critically for us, he also shows that students study less for courses offered *by* departments with more lenient grading standards.

22. There is one important silver lining to the fact that UCSB's URM and low-income students are being eased out of the majors in highest demand. The number of (more-advantaged) students in humanities and humanistic social science majors that URM and low-income students do tend to complete have decreased, but their faculty numbers in these majors have not. As a consequence, they offer substantially better faculty-student ratios and smaller classes. The greater individualized attention that this makes possible is particularly important for students who need to make up for gaps in their high school education. Ensuring that faculty hiring in these disciplines remains robust despite the outmigration of majors is therefore important.

23. The evidence of increasing inequality of outcomes at UCSB doesn't necessarily imply inequality of opportunities. It may be the case that students of different backgrounds have different outcomes because they make different choices. We are aware of this possibility because there is good evidence that students of different backgrounds do make different major choices. See Eric Eide

and Geetha Waehrer, "The Role of the Option Value of College Attendance in College Major Choice," *Economics of Education Review* 17, no. 1 (1998): 73–82; J. Farley Ordovensky Staniec, "The Effects of Race, Sex, and Expected Returns on the Choice of College Major," *Eastern Economic Journal* 30, no. 4 (2004): 549–562; Peter Arcidiacono, V. Joseph Hotz, and Songman Kang, "Modeling College Major Choices Using Elicited Measures of Expectations and Counterfactuals," *Journal of Econometrics* 166, no. 1 (2012): 3–16; and Matthew Wiswall and Basit Zafar, "Determinants of College Major Choice: Identification using an Information Experiment," *Review of Economic Studies* 82, no. 2 (2015): 791–824.

24. We derived these results from an event study, a comparison across majors and over time of some outcomes. In this case, we compared the number of majors, the number of majors who are URMs, the SAT scores of majors who are URMs, and the first-year GPAs of majors who are URMs. By controlling for the level of a particular outcome in the same year on the same campus and its average value in the major on that campus over time, we could assess how much this outcome differed from its expected level in the years before and after the pre-major was introduced. We found that the number of students in a typical major rose above predicted levels before pre-majors were introduced but that the introduction of a pre-major reduced that number on average by 10% right after it was introduced. Similarly, the proportion of students who were URMs decreased by around 2–3%, while the average SAT score of majors increased 200 points and their average freshman GPA rose 0.32 points on a 4-point scale.

25. They estimate that 32% of Davis students who have taken Economics 1 completed an economics major, compared with 26% at UCSB.

26. See Zachary Bleemer and Aashish Mehta, "College Major Restrictions and Student Stratification," Center for Studies in Higher Education Research and Occasional Papers 21, no. 14 (2021), https://cshe.berkeley.edu/publications/college-major-restrictions-and-student-stratification-zachary-bleemer-and-aashish-mehta. A key problem with the standard wage-by-major statistics is that they compare the wages earned by people who chose to major in one field to the wages earned by a completely different set of people who chose to major in another field. Such a comparison cannot tell us what randomly switching one of these people to the other group's major would have done to their earnings. In contrast, when we studied the effects of rejection from a restricted major, we actually compared the wages of two groups of people who (a) both displayed some interest in the major in question, and (b) were, for all intents and purposes, randomly assigned to that major or to some others; see Zachary Bleemer and Aashish Mehta, "Will Studying Economics Make You Rich? A Regression Discontinuity Analysis of the Returns to College Major," *American Economic Journal: Applied Economics* 14, no. 2 (2022): 1–22. It is possible to learn about the effects of rejecting interested students from a major through such a comparison. We did this by comparing the wages of a group of people who had just about managed to

earn the lowest GPA that gave them entry into a major with the wages of people who studied on the same campus but failed to earn that GPA. These groups should be otherwise very similar.

27. Richard Sabot and John Wakeman-Linn, "Grade Inflation and Course Choice," *Journal of Economic Perspectives* 5, no. 1 (1991): 159–170; Kristin F. Butcher, Patrick J. McEwan, and Akila Weerapana, "The Effects of an Anti-Grade-Inflation Policy at Wellesley College," *Journal of Economic Perspectives* 28, no. 3 (2014): 189–204.

28. Robert Kelchen provides a spreadsheet with six-year graduation rate data for Pell Grant recipients and for all other students (and some caveats about their quality); see "New Data on Pell Grant Recipients' Graduation Rates," Robert Kelchen (blog), February 18, 2019, https://robertkelchen.com/2019/02/18/new-data-on-pell-grant-recipients-graduation-rates/. More recent data on eight-year graduation rates are available from the US Department of Education's College Scorecard (https://collegescorecard.ed.gov).

29. Elizabeth A. Armstrong and Laura T. Hamilton, *Paying for the Party: How College Maintains Inequality* (Cambridge, MA: Harvard University Press, 2013).

Conclusion

Epigraph: Quoted in Carlos Spoerhase, "Rankings: A Pre-History," New Left Review 114 (2018).

1. Thorstein Veblen, *The Theory of the Leisure Class* (1899; repr., New York: Penguin, 1994), 394 ("priestly," "magical," "archaic"), 383 ("merely useful," "classics").

2. Thorstein Veblen, *The Higher Learning in America* (1918; repr., Baltimore: Johns Hopkins University Press), 147.

3. Veblen, *The Higher Learning in America*, 53.

4. Philip Mirowski and Esther-Mirjam Sent, "Introduction," in *Science Bought and Sold: Essays in the Economics of Science*, edited by Philip Mirowski and Esther-Mirjam Sent (Chicago: University of Chicago Press, 2002).

5. Christopher Newfield, *The Great Mistake: How We Wrecked Public Universities and How We Can Fix Them* (Baltimore: Johns Hopkins University Press, 2016).

6. It is not our intention to be nostalgic about a university of the past, especially because it was an elite institution that discriminated against and excluded many women and racial and ethnic minorities.

7. Wendy Brown, *Undoing the Demos: Neoliberalism's Stealth Revolution* (New York: Zone Books, 2015).

8. Vinay Gidwani and Rajyashree N. Reddy provide a nice summary of Locke's ideas in relation to waste; see "The Afterlives of 'Waste': Notes from India for a Minor History of Capitalist Surplus," *Antipode* 43, no. 5 (2011): 1625–1658.

9. Arguments that universities are wasteful in the sense of inefficiency are widespread. For a criticism from inside the university, see Benjamin Ginsberg, *Fall of the Faculty: The Rise of the All-Administrative University and Why It Matters* (Oxford: Oxford University Press, 2011). For a criticism from two business consultants, see Jeff Denneen and Tom Dretler, *The Financially Sustainable University* (Chicago: Sterling Partners and Bain & Co., 2012). For critiques of wasteful universities from the political right, see Richard Vedder, *Going Broke by Degree: Why College Costs Too Much* (Washington DC: American Enterprise Institute Press, 2004); and Bryan Caplan, *The Case against Education: Why the Education System Is a Waste of Time and Money* (Princeton, NJ: Princeton University Press, 2018).

10. Christopher Newfield, *The Great Mistake: How We Wrecked Public Universities and How We Can Fix Them* (Baltimore: Johns Hopkins University Press, 2016).

11. See American Association of University Professions, "The Annual Report on the Economic Status of the Profession, 2020–21," July 2021, https://www .aaup.org/file/AAUP_ARES_2020-21.pdf; OECD, *Education at a Glance 2018: OECD Indicators* (Paris: OECD Publishing, 2018); Higher Education Statistics Agency, "Higher Education Staff Statistics: UK, 2016/17," January 18, 2018, https://www.hesa.ac.uk/news/18-01-2018/sfr248-higher-education-staff -statistics; Ginsberg, *Fall of the Faculty*.

12. Marcus A. Doel, "Miserly Thinking / Excessful Geography: From Restricted Economy to Global Financial Crisis," *Environment and Planning D: Society and Space* 27, no. 6 (2009): 1054–1073.

13. M. Strathern, "'Improving Ratings': Audit in the British University System," *European Review* 5, no. 3 (1997): 305321.

14. Eric Archambault and Vincent Lariviere, "History of the Journal Impact Factor: Contingencies and Consequences," *Scientometrics* 79, no. 3 (2009): 635–649.

Bibliography

Alterman, Eric. "The Decline of Historical Thinking." *New Yorker*, February 4, 2019. https://www.newyorker.com/news/news-desk/the-decline-of -historical-thinking.

Altonji, Joseph, Peter Arcidiacono, and Arnaud Maurel. "The Analysis of Field Choice in College and Graduate School: Determinants and Wage Effects." *Handbook of the Economics of Education* 5 (2016): 305–396.

American Academy of Arts and Sciences. *The State of the Humanities 2018: Graduates in the Workforce & Beyond.* Cambridge, MA: American Academy of Arts and Sciences, 2018.

American Association of University Professions. "The Annual Report on the Economic Status of the Profession, 2020–21." July 2021. https://www.aaup .org/file/AAUP_ARES_2020-21.pdf.

American Institutes for Research. "In Minnesota, Majors Matter, AIR Study Finds; Future Earnings Linked to College Course of Study." AIR, October 4, 2016. Accessed May 2018. https://www.air.org/news/press-release/minnesota -majors-matter-air-study-finds-future-earnings-linked-college-course.

Anwar, Yasmin. "UC Berkeley Still No.1 Public, Fourth Best Globally in U.S. News Rankings." UC Berkeley, October 20, 2020. https://news.berkeley.edu/2020 /10/20/uc-berkeley-still-no-1-public-fourth-best-globally-in-u-s-news -rankings/.

Archambault, Eric, and Vincent Lariviere. "History of the Journal Impact Factor: Contingencies and Consequences." *Scientometrics* 79, no. 3 (2009): 635–649.

Arcidiacono, Peter. "Ability Sorting and the Returns to College Major." *Journal of Econometrics* 121, nos. 1–2 (2004): 343–375.

Arcidiacono, Peter, V. Joseph Hotz, and Songman Kang. "Modeling College Major Choices Using Elicited Measures of Expectations and Counterfactuals." *Journal of Econometrics* 166, no. 1 (2012): 3–16.

Armstrong, Elizabeth A., and Laura T. Hamilton. *Paying for the Party: How College Maintains Inequality.* Cambridge, MA: Harvard University Press, 2013.

Arum, Richard, and Josipa Roksa. *Academically Adrift: Limited Learning on College Campuses*. Chicago: University of Chicago Press, 2011.

Babcock, Philip. "Real Costs of Nominal Grade Inflation? New Evidence from Student Course Evaluations." *Economic Inquiry* 48, no. 4 (2010): 983–996.

Bakula, Marta. "Record-Low Acceptance Rate as Applicant Numbers Increase." *Chicago Maroon*, April 14, 2015. https://www.chicagomaroon.com/2015/04 /14/record-low-acceptance-rate-as-applicant-numbers-increase/.

Bartik, Alexander, and Scott T. Nelson. "Credit Reports as Resumes: The Incidence of Pre-Employment Credit Screening." *MIT Department of Economics Graduate Student Research Papers* 16, no. 01, March 7, 2016.

Baum, Sandy, and Jennifer Ma. *Trends in College Pricing, 2013*. New York: The College Board, 2013.

Berman, Elizabeth Popp, and Abby Stivers. "Student Loans as a Pressure on U.S. Higher Education." In *The University under Pressure*, ed. Elizabeth Popp Berman and Catherine Paradeise, 129–160. Bingley, UK: Emerald Publishing, 2016.

Best, Joel, and Eric Best. *The Student Loan Mess: How Good Intentions Created a Trillion-Dollar Problem*. Berkeley: University of California Press, 2014.

Black, Sandra E., Jeffrey T. Denning, and Jesse Rothstein. "Winners and Losers? The Effect of Gaining and Losing Access to Selective Colleges on Education and Labor Market Outcomes." National Bureau of Economic Research Working Paper 26821, March 2020. https://www.nber.org/system/files /working_papers/w26821/w26821.pdf.

Bleemer, Zachary. "Affirmative Action, Mismatch, and Economic Mobility after California's Proposition 209." *Quarterly Journal of Economics* 137, no. 1 (2022): 115–160.

———. "Top Percent Policies and the Return to Postsecondary Selectivity." Center for Studies in Higher Education Research and Occasional Papers 21, no. 1, January 2021. https://cshe.berkeley.edu/publications/top-percent-policies -and-return-postsecondary-selectivity-zachary-bleemer-cshe-121.

———. "The UC ClioMetric History Project and Formatted Optical Character Recognition." Center for Studies in Higher Education Research and Occasional Papers 18, no. 3, 2018. https://cshe.berkeley.edu/publications/uc -cliometric-history-project-and-formatted-optical-character-recognition -zachary.

Bleemer, Zachary, Meta Brown, Donghoon Lee, Katherine Strair, and Wilbert van der Klaauw. "Echoes of Rising Tuition in Students' Borrowing, Educational Attainment, and Homeownership in Post-Recession America." *Journal of Urban Economics* 122 (2021): 103298.

Bleemer, Zachary, Meta Brown, Donghoon Lee, and Wilbert van der Klaauw. "Tuition, Jobs, or Housing: What's Keeping Millennials at Home?" *Federal Reserve Bank of New York Staff Reports* 700, November 2014.

Bleemer, Zachary, and Aashish Mehta. "College Major Restrictions and Student Stratification." Center for Studies in Higher Education Research and Occasional Papers 21, no. 14 (2021). https://cshe.berkeley.edu/publications /college-major-restrictions-and-student-stratification-zachary-bleemer-and -aashish-mehta.

———. "Will Studying Economics Make You Rich? A Regression Discontinuity Analysis of the Returns to College Major." *American Economic Journal: Applied Economics* 14, no. 2 (2022): 1–22.

Bleemer, Zachary, and Basit Zafar. "Intended College Attendance: Evidence from an Experiment on College Returns and Costs." *Journal of Public Economics* 157 (2018): 184–211.

Bound, John, Charles Brown, and Nancy Mathiowetz. "Measurement Error in Survey Data." *Handbook of Econometrics* 5 (2001): 3705–3843.

Bowen, William G., Matthew M. Chingos, and Michael S. McPherson. *Crossing the Finish Line: Completing College at America's Public Universities.* Princeton, NJ: Princeton University Press, 2009.

Breen, Richard, Seongsoo Choi, Anders Holmb. "Heterogeneous Causal Effects and Sample Selection Bias." *Sociological Science* 2 (2016): 351–369.

Brown, Wendy. *Undoing the Demos: Neoliberalism's Stealth Revolution.* New York: Zone Books, 2015.

Bureau of Education. *Biennial Survey of Education: 1920–1922.* Washington, DC: Government Printing Office, 1925.

Bryant, Gareth, and Ben Spies-Butcher. "Bringing Finance Inside the State: How Income-Contingent Loans Blur the Boundaries between Debt and Tax." *Environment and Planning A: Economy & Space* 52, no. 1 (2020): 111–129.

Butcher, Kristin F., Patrick J. McEwan, and Akila Weerapana. "The Effects of an Anti-Grade-Inflation Policy at Wellesley College." *Journal of Economic Perspectives* 28, no. 3 (2014): 189–204.

Caplan, Bryan. *The Case against Education: Why the Education System Is a Waste of Time and Money.* Princeton, NJ: Princeton University Press, 2018.

Carnevale, Anthony P., Ban Cheah, and Andrew R. Hanson. *The Economic Value of College Majors.* Washington, DC: Georgetown University Center on Education and the Workforce, 2015.

Carnevale, Anthony, Ban Cheah, and Martin Van Der Werf. *A First Try at ROI: Ranking 4,500 Colleges.* Washington, DC: Georgetown University Center on Education and the Workforce, 2019.

Carnevale, Anthony P., and Jeff Strohl. *Separate & Unequal.* Washington, DC: Georgetown University Center on Education and the Workforce, 2013. https://1gyhoq479ufd3yna29x7ubjn-wpengine.netdna-ssl.com/wp-content /uploads/SeparateUnequal.ES_.pdf.

Center for Microeconomic Data. *Quarterly Report on Household Debt and Credit: 2021 Q1.* New York: New York Federal Reserve Bank, 2021. https://www

.newyorkfed.org/medialibrary/interactives/householdcredit/data/pdf/HHDC
_2021Q1.pdf.

Chetty, Raj, John N. Friedman, Emmanuel Saez, Nicholas Turner, and Danny
Yagan. "Income Segregation and Intergenerational Mobility across Colleges
in the United States." *Quarterly Journal of Economics* 135, no. 3 (2020):
1567–1633.

———. "Mobility Report Cards: The Role of Colleges in Intergenerational
Mobility." National Bureau of Economic Research Working Papers 23618,
July 2017. https://www.nber.org/papers/w23618.

Clark, Damon, and Heather Royer. "The Effect of Education on Adult Mortality
and Health: Evidence from Britain." *American Economic Review* 103, no. 6
(2013): 2087–2120.

Clark, Kim. "How Money Ranked the 2016 Best Colleges." *Money*, July 11, 2016.
https://money.com/how-money-ranks-best-colleges-2016/.

Coffey, Randon. "U.S. News & World Report Names Cottey College the Best in the
Midwest Region." Cottey College, September 14, 2020. https://cottey.edu
/2020/09/rankings/#:~:text=COVID%2D19-,U.S.%20NEWS%20%26%20
WORLD%20REPORT%20NAMES%20COTTEY%20COLLEGE,BEST%20
IN%20THE%20MIDWEST%20REGION&text=NEVADA%2C%20MO%E2
%80%94Today%2C%20U.S.,states%20comprising%20the%20Midwest%20
region.

Cohen, Patricia. "A Rising Call to Promote STEM Education and Cut Liberal Arts
Funding." *New York Times*, February 21, 2016. https://www.nytimes.com
/2016/02/22/business/a-rising-call-to-promote-stem-education-and-cut
-liberal-arts-funding.html.

Cohodes, Sarah R., and Joshua S. Goodman. "Merit Aid, College Quality, and
College Completion: Massachusetts' Adams Scholarship as an In-Kind
Subsidy." *American Economic Journal: Applied Economics* 6, no. 4 (2014):
251–285.

College Board. *Trends in College Pricing and Student Aid 2020*. New York: College
Board, 2020.

Columbia University, Financial Aid & Educational Financing. "Facts and Figures."
[2002]. https://cc-seas.financialaid.columbia.edu/eligibility/facts.

Conklin, Thomas, and Christa Gibbs. *Data Point: Borrower Experiences on
Income-Driven Repayment*. Washington, DC: Consumer Financial Protection
Bureau, 2019. https://files.consumerfinance.gov/f/documents/cfpb_data
-point_borrower-experiences-on-IDR.pdf.

Dale, Stacy, and Alan Krueger. "Estimating the Effects of College Characteristics
over the Career Using Administrative Earnings Data." *Journal of Human
Resources* 49, no. 2 (2014): 323–358.

Dee, Thomas. "Are There Civic Returns to Education?" *Journal of Public Economics*
88, nos. 9–10 (2004): 1697–1720.

Deming, David, and Christopher Walters. "The Impact of Price Caps and Spending Cuts on U.S. Postsecondary Attainment." National Bureau of Economic Research Working Papers 23736. August 2017. https://www.nber.org /papers/w23736.

Denneen, Jeff, and Tom Dretler. *The Financially Sustainable University*. Chicago: Sterling Partners and Bain & Co., 2012.

Desrochers, Donna M., Colleen M. Lenihan, and Jane V. Wellman. *Trends in College Spending, 1998–2008: Where Does the Money Come From? Where Does It Go? What Does It Buy?* Washington, D.C.: Delta Cost Project, 2019.

Diamond, Rebecca, and Enrico Moretti. "Where Is Standard of Living the Highest? Local Prices and the Geography of Consumption." National Bureau of Economic Research Working Papers 29533, December 2021. https://www .nber.org/papers/w29533.

Doel, Marcus A. "Miserly Thinking/Excessful Geography: From Restricted Economy to Global Financial Crisis." *Environment and Planning D: Society and Space* 27, no. 6 (2009): 1054–1073.

Durkin, Karen. "Gallaudet University Named No. 3 in the Nation for 'Best Value Schools' in U.S. News & World Report 2021 Best Colleges Rankings." PRWeb, September 14, 2020. Accessed June 2021. https://www.prweb.com /releases/gallaudet_university_named_no_3_in_the_nation_for_best_value _schools_in_u_s_news_world_report_2021_best_colleges_rankings/prweb 17390875.htm#:~:text=Today%20Gallaudet%20University%20was%20 recognized,the%20same%20category%20l.

Dynarski, Susan, C. J. Libassi, Katherine Michelmore, and Stephanie Owen. "Closing the Gap: The Effect of Reducing Complexity and Uncertainty in College Pricing on the Choices of Low-Income Students." *American Economic Review* 111, no. 6 (2021): 1721–1756.

Eaton, Charlie. "Still Public: State Universities and America's New Student-Debt Coalitions." *PS: Political Science & Politics* 50, no. 2 (2017): 408–412.

Eide, Eric, and Geetha Waehrer. "The Role of the Option Value of College Attendance in College Major Choice." *Economics of Education Review* 17, no. 1 (1998): 73–82.

Feeney, Matt. "The Pointless End of Legacy Admissions." *New Yorker*, November 23, 2021. https://www.newyorker.com/culture/cultural-comment/the -pointless-end-of-legacy-admissions.

Ferrier, William W. *Origin and Development of the University of California*. Berkeley, CA: The Sather Gate Book Shop, 1930.

First, Zachary. "When the Humanities Are Worth It." PayScale, November 11, 2016. https://www.payscale.com/career-news/2016/11/what-major-should-i-choose.

Foreman, Liz, and Ashley Corinne Killough. "Freshmen Get $300 to Retake the SAT." *Baylor Lariat*, October 10, 2008. https://www.baylor.edu/content /services/document.php?id=73959.

Fuller, Carol, and Carlo Salerno. *Information Required to Be Disclosed Under the Higher Education Act of 1965: Suggestions for Dissemination (Updated)*. NPEC 2010-831v2. Washington, DC: National Postsecondary Education Collective, 2009.

Fung Bros. "UC Stereotypes Explained: UCLA, UCB, UCR, UCI etc." YouTube video, September 11, 2014. https://www.youtube.com/watch?v=int3lFioTtU.

Gallup and Purdue University. *Great Jobs, Great Lives: The 2014 Gallup-Purdue Index Report*. Washington, DC: Gallup, 2014. https://www.gallup.com /services/176768/2014-gallup-purdue-index-report.aspx.

Gidwani, Vinay, and Rajyashree N. Reddy. "The Afterlives of 'Waste': Notes from India for a Minor History of Capitalist Surplus." *Antipode* 43, no. 5 (2011): 1625–1658.

Ginsberg, Benjamin. *Fall of the Faculty: The Rise of the All-Administrative University and Why It Matters*. Oxford: Oxford University Press, 2011.

Goldin, Claudia, Lawrence F. Katz, and Ilyana Kuziemko. "The Homecoming of American College Women: The Reversal of the College Gender Gap." *Journal of Economic Perspectives* 20, no. 4 (2006): 133–156.

Goldrick-Rab, Sara. *Paying the Price: College Costs, Financial Aid, and the Betrayal of the American Dream*. Chicago: University of Chicago Press, 2016.

Graeber, David. *Debt: The First 5,000 Years*. Brooklyn, NY: Melville House, 2011.

Gurantz, Oded, Jessica Howell, Michael Hurwitz, Cassandra Larson, Matea Pender, and Brooke White. "A National-Level Information Experiment to Promote Enrollment in Selective Universities." *Journal of Policy Analysis and Management* 40, no. 2 (2021): 453–479.

Hayden, Tyler. "UCSB Course Shortage at 'Crisis' Level, Dean Says." *Santa Barbara Independent*, September 15, 2021. https://www.independent.com/2021/09 /15/ucsb-course-shortage-at-crisis-level-dean-says/.

Hershbein, Brad J. "Worker Signals among New College Graduates: The Role of Selectivity and GPA." Upjohn Institute Working Papers 13, no. 190. January 1, 2013. https://research.upjohn.org/up_workingpapers/190/.

Higher Education Statistics Agency. "Higher Education Staff Statistics: UK, 2016/17." January 18, 2018. https://www.hesa.ac.uk/news/18-01-2018 /sfr248-higher-education-staff-statistics.

Hoover, Eric. "Application Inflation: When Is Enough Enough?" *New York Times*, November 5, 2010. https://www.chronicle.com/article/application-inflation/. https://www.nytimes.com/2010/11/07/education/edlife/07HOOVER-t.html.

Hoxby, Caroline, and Christopher Avery. "The Missing 'One-Offs': The Hidden Supply of High-Achieving, Low-Income Students." Brookings Papers on Economic Activity 2013, no. 1 (2013): 1–65.

Hoxby, Caroline, and Sarah Turner. "Expanding College Opportunities for High-Achieving, Low Income Students." Stanford Institute for Economic

Policy Research Discussion Papers 12, no. 14, March 2013. https://siepr
.stanford.edu/publications/working-paper/expanding-college-opportunities
-high-achieving-low-income-students.

———. "Measuring Opportunity in Higher Education." National Bureau of
Economic Research Working Papers 25479. January 2019. https://www.nber
.org/system/files/working_papers/w25479/w25479.pdf.

Immordino-Yang, Mary Helen. "Studying the Effects of Culture by Integrating
Neuroscientific with Ethnographic Approaches." *Psychological Inquiry* 24,
no. 1 (2013): 42–46. https://doi.org/10.1080/1047840X.2013.770278.

Jackson, Abby. "The 3 Most Popular Majors at Every Ivy League School." Insider,
February 16, 2018. https://www.businessinsider.com/most-popular-ivy
-league-major-2017-4.

Jaschik, Scott. "Apology from Obama." *Inside Higher Ed*, February 19, 2014.
https://www.insidehighered.com/news/2014/02/19/professor-art-history
-receives-handwritten-apology-president-obama.

Jeszeck, Charles A. "Older Americans: Inability to Repay Student Loans May
Affect Financial Security of a Small Percentage of Retirees." Testimony before
the Special Committee on Aging, U.S. Senate. Washington, DC: GAO, 2014.
https://www.gao.gov/assets/gao-14-866t.pdf.

Juszkiewicz, Jolanta. *Trends in Community College Enrollment and Completion
Data, 2016*. Washington, DC: American Association of Community Colleges,
2016.

Kelchen, Robert. "New Data on Pell Grant Recipients' Graduation Rates." Robert
Kelchen (blog), February 18, 2019. https://robertkelchen.com/2019/02/18
/new-data-on-pell-grant-recipients-graduation-rates/.

Kirkeboen, Lars J., Edwin Leuven, and Magne Mogstad. "Field of Study, Earnings,
and Self-Selection." *Quarterly Journal of Economics* 131, no. 3 (2016):
1057–1111.

Kim, HoonHo, and Diane Lalancette. *Literature Review on the Value-Added
Measurement in Higher Education*. Paris: Organisation for Economic
Cooperation and Development, 2013.

Korn, Melissa, and Jennifer Levitz. *Unacceptable: Privilege, Deceit & the Making of
the College Admissions Scandal*. New York: Portfolio/Penguin, 2020.

Kreznar, Christian, ed. "America's Top Colleges: The First Time a Public School Is
Number One." 2022. https://www.forbes.com/top-colleges/.

Kutner, Max. "How to Game the College Rankings." *Boston*, August 26, 2014.
https://www.bostonmagazine.com/news/2014/08/26/how-northeastern
-gamed-the-college-rankings/.

Lederman, Doug. "'Manipulating,' Er, Influencing 'U.S. News.'" *Inside Higher Ed*,
June 3, 2009. https://www.insidehighered.com/news/2009/06/03
/manipulating-er-influencing-us-news.

———. "PayScale's Impact (and Limitations)." *Inside Higher Ed*, April 18, 2017. https://www.insidehighered.com/news/2017/04/18/payscale-rankings-roi -have-influence-and-significant-limitations.

Leonhardt, David. "Getting a Clearer Picture of College Costs." Economix, September 18, 2013. https://economix.blogs.nytimes.com/2013/09/18 /getting-a-clearer-picture-of-college-costs/.

———. "A Simpler Financial-Aid Calculator Spreads." *New York Times*, September 21, 2015. https://www.nytimes.com/2015/09/22/upshot/a-simpler -financial-aid-calculator-spreads.html.

———. "Top Colleges Are Cheaper than You Think (Unless You're Rich)." *New York Times*, June 5, 2018. https://www.nytimes.com/interactive/2018/06 /05/opinion/columnists/what-college-really-costs.html.

Levine, Phillip B. "Transparency in College Costs." Economic Studies Working Paper, November 2014. Brookings Institution, Washington, DC.

Levine, Phillip B., Jennifer Ma, and Lauren C. Russell. "Do College Applicants Respond to Changes in Sticker Prices Even When They Don't Matter?" National Bureau of Economic Research Working Papers 26910, March 2020. https://www.nber.org/papers/w26910.

Levy, Jeff. "The Great 'Success' of the University of Chicago." BigJ Educational Consulting, July 10, 2019, https://www.bigjeducationalconsulting.com/blog /finding-colleges-that-are-affordable.s

Lochner, Lance, and Enrico Moretti. "The Effect of Education on Crime: Evidence from Prison Inmates, Arrests, and Self-Reports." *American Economic Review* 94, no. 1 (2004): 155–189.

Luca, Michael, and Jonathan Smith. "Salience in Quality Disclosure: Evidence from the U.S. News College Rankings." *Journal of Economics & Management Strategy* 22, no. 1 (2013): 58–77.

Lucca, David O., Taylor Nadauld, and Karen Shen. "Credit Supply and the Rise in College Tuition: Evidence from the Expansion in Federal Student Aid Programs." *Review of Financial Studies* 32, no. 2 (2019): 423–466.

McClanahan, Annie. *Dead Pledges: Debt, Crisis, and Twenty-First-Century Culture*. Stanford, CA: Stanford University Press, 2017.

———. "The Living Indebted: Student Militancy and the Financialization of Debt." *Qui Parle* 20, no. 1 (2011): 57–77.

McGettigan, Andrew. *The Great University Gamble*. London: Pluto Press, 2013.

McLean, Bethany. "Sallie Mae: A Hot Stock, a Tough Lender." *CNN Money*, December 14, 2005. https://money.cnn.com/2005/12/14/news/fortune500 /sallie_fortune_122605/index.htm.

McMahon, Walter. *Higher Learning, Greater Good*. Baltimore, MD: Johns Hopkins University Press, 2009.

Meister, Bob. "Debt and Taxes: Can the Financial Industry Save Public Universities?" *Representations* 116, no. 1 (2011): 128–155.

Meranze, Michael, and Christopher Newfield. "UCLA Loses Loni: Why Budget Silence Is Bad for Science." Remaking the University, May 12, 2013. http://utotherescue.blogspot.com/2013/05/ucla-loses-loni-why-budget-silence-is.html.

Mirowski, Philip, and Esther-Mirjam Sent. "Introduction." In *Science Bought and Sold: Essays in the Economics of Science*, edited by Philip Mirowski and Esther-Mirjam Sent. Chicago: University of Chicago Press, 2002.

Mok, Harry. "9 UC Campuses Ranked among World's Best Universities." University of California, August 15, 2014. https://www.universityofcalifornia.edu/news/9-uc-campuses-ranked-among-world%E2%80%99s-best-universities.

Moretti, Enrico. "Estimating the Social Return to Higher Education: Evidence from Longitudinal and Repeated Cross-Sectional Data." *Journal of Econometrics* 121 (2004): 175–212.

———. "Workers' Education, Spillovers, and Productivity: Evidence from Plant-Level Production Functions." *American Economic Review* 94, no. 3 (2004): 656–690.

Morse, Robert, and Eric Brooks. "A More Detailed Look at the Ranking Factors." *U.S. News*, September 12, 2021. https://www.usnews.com/education/best-colleges/articles/ranking-criteria-and-weights.

National Academy of Sciences, National Academy of Engineering, and Institute of Medicine. *Rising above the Gathering Storm*. Washington, DC: National Academies Press, 2007.

———. *Rising above the Gathering Storm, Revisited*. Washington, DC: National Academies Press, 2010.

National Center for Education Statistics. "Postsecondary Institution Expenses." Last updated May 2021. https://nces.ed.gov/programs/coe/indicator/cue.

———. "Undergraduate Retention and Graduation Rates." Last updated May 2022. https://nces.ed.gov/programs/coe/indicator/ctr.

Newfield, Christopher. *The Great Mistake: How We Wrecked Public Universities and How We Can Fix Them*. Baltimore: Johns Hopkins University Press, 2016.

Obama, Barack. "Remarks by the President on College Affordability—Buffalo, NY." August 23, 2013. https://obamawhitehouse.archives.gov/the-press-office/2013/08/22/remarks-president-college-affordability-buffalo-ny.

OECD. *Education at a Glance 2018: OECD Indicators*. Paris: OECD Publishing, 2018. https://www.oecd-ilibrary.org/docserver/eag-2018-en.pdf?expires=1657638296&id=id&accname=guest&checksum=AEAD62E3247D13AEDE259B552B8838FB.

Rimer, Sara. "Baylor Rewards Freshmen Who Retake SAT." *New York Times*, October 14, 2008. https://www.nytimes.com/2008/10/15/education/15baylor.html.

Ruggles, Steven, Sarah Flood, Ronald Goeken, Josiah Grover, Erin Meyer, Jose Pacas, and Matthew Sobek. "U.S. Census Data for Social, Economic, and Health Research." 2020. https://usa.ipums.org/usa/.

Sabot, Richard, and John Wakeman-Linn. "Grade Inflation and Course Choice." *Journal of Economic Perspectives* 5, no. 1 (1991): 159–170.

Sandel, Michael. *What Money Can't Buy: The Moral Limits of Markets*. New York: Farrar, Straus and Giroux, 2012.

Seltzer, Rick. "Return on Students' Investments Varies over Time." *Insider Higher Ed*, November 14, 2019. https://www.insidehighered.com/news/2019/11/14/differences-college-roi-vary-institution-type-and-time-frame-measured-report-says.

Shavit, Yossi, Richard Arum, and Adam Gamoran. *Stratification in Higher Education: A Comparative Study*. Stanford, CA: Stanford University Press, 2017.

Spoerhase, Carlos. "Rankings: A Pre-History." *New Left Review* 114 (2018): 99–112.

Staniec, J. Farley Ordovensky. "The Effects of Race, Sex, and Expected Returns on the Choice of College Major." *Eastern Economic Journal* 30, no. 4 (2004): 549–562.

Steele, James B., and Lance Williams. "Who Got Rich Off the Student Debt Crisis?" *Reveal*, June 28, 2016. https://revealnews.org/article/who-got-rich-off-the-student-debt-crisis/.

Stinebrickner, Ralph, and Todd R. Stinebrickner. "A Major in Science? Initial Beliefs and Final Outcomes for College Major and Dropout." *Review of Economic Studies* 81, no. 1 (2014): 426–472.

Strathern, M. "'Improving Ratings': Audit in the British University System." *European Review* 5, no. 3 (1997): 305321.

Strauss, Valerie. "U.S. News Changed the Way It Ranks Colleges. It's Still Ridiculous." *Washington Post*, September 12, 2018. https://www.washingtonpost.com/education/2018/09/12/us-news-changed-way-it-ranks-colleges-its-still-ridiculous/.

Strike Debt. *The Debt Resisters' Operations Manual*. Oakland, CA: PM Press, 2014. https://strikedebt.org/drom/#toc.

Tough, Paul. "Who Gets to Graduate?" *New York Times*, May 15, 2014. http://www.nytimes.com/2014/05/18/magazine/who-gets-to-graduate.html.

———. *The Years that Matter Most: How College Makes or Breaks Us*. Boston, MA: Houghton Mifflin Harcourt, 2019.

University of California. "Undergraduate Admissions Summary." 2021. https://www.universityofcalifornia.edu/about-us/information-center/admissions-residency-and-ethnicity.

Urban Institute. "Understanding College Affordability: How Students, Institutions, and the Public Pay for Higher Education." 2017. http://collegeaffordability.urban.org.

U.S. Department of Education College Scorecard. "Columbia University in the City of New York." Last updated May 2, 2022. https://collegescorecard.ed.gov/school/?190150-Columbia-University-in-the-City-of-New-York.

———. "Find the Right Fit." Last updated May 2, 2022. https://collegescorecard
.ed.gov/.

———. "Pace University." Last updated June 15, 2022. https://collegescorecard
.ed.gov/school/?194310-Pace-University.

———. "SUNY at Albany." Last updated June 15, 2022. https://collegescorecard
.ed.gov/school/?196060-SUNY-at-Albany.

U.S. Department of Education Press Office. "Secretary DeVos Delivers on Promise
to Provide Students Relevant, Actionable Information Needed to Make
Personalized Education Decisions." U.S. Department of Education Press
Office, November 20, 2019. https://content.govdelivery.com/accounts
/USED/bulletins/26d1286.

U.S. Senate Subcommittee on Health, Employment, Labor, and Pensions. *For Profit
Higher Education: The Failure to Safeguard the Federal Investment and Ensure
Student Success*. Vol. 1 of 4. Washington, DC: Government Printing Office,
2012. https://www.govinfo.gov/content/pkg/CPRT-112SPRT74931/pdf
/CPRT-112SPRT74931.pdf.

Veblen, Thorstein. *The Higher Learning in America*. 1918; repr., Baltimore: Johns
Hopkins University Press.

———. *The Theory of the Leisure Class*. 1899; repr., New York: Penguin, 1994.

Vedder, Richard. *Going Broke by Degree: Why College Costs Too Much*. Washington
DC: American Enterprise Institute Press, 2004.

White House, Office of the Press Secretary. "Remarks by the President on
Opportunity for All and Skills for America's Workers." Waukesha, Wisconsin.
January 30, 2014. https://obamawhitehouse.archives.gov/the-press-office
/2014/01/30/remarks-president-opportunity-all-and-skills-americas-workers.

Wiswall, Matthew, and Basit Zafar. "Determinants of College Major Choice:
Identification using an Information Experiment." *Review of Economic Studies*
82, no. 2 (2015): 791–824.

———. "Preference for the Workplace, Human Capital, and Gender." National
Bureau of Economic Research Working Papers 22173, April 2016. https://
www.nber.org/papers/w22173.

World University Rankings. "Wall Street Journal/Times Higher Education College
Rankings 2018." https://www.timeshighereducation.com/rankings/united
-states/2018#!/page/0/length/25/sort_by/rank/sort_order/asc/cols/stats.

Zaloom, Caitlin. *Indebted: How Families Make College Work at Any Cost*. Princeton,
NJ: Princeton University Press, 2019.

Zhou, Enyu, and Pilar Mendoza. "Financing Higher Education in the United
States: A Historical Overview of Loans in Federal Financial Aid Policy." In
The Neoliberal Agenda and the Student Debt Crisis in U.S. Higher Education,
ed. Nicholas D. Hartlep, Lucille L. T. Eckrich, and Brandon O. Hensley,
3–18. New York: Routledge, 2017.

Index

high-wage graduates, 141. *See also* average wages by college major

economics majors: high average wages for, 95, 98–99, 105, 161n28; restrictions on, 93, 126–27, 128; student preference for, 98

electives, 130

Eligibility in Local Context (ELC) Program, 26–28, 29

engineering: earnings in, 17, 85, 86, 88, 89–90, 95, *108*, 112; entry requirements for, 93; restrictions on majors in, 114, 128

English majors, 98, 111

federal grants: Pell Grants, 117, 129, 162n6, 163n8; universities become dependent on, 137

financial aid: calculators for, 65–68; at Columbia, 54, 70; credit requirements for, 119; graduation rates and, 46–47; for lower-income students, 61, 63, 69; "sticker price" and, 56, 58, 60; student debt and, 6

First, Zachary, 12–13

Forbes, 13, 16, 57

Georgetown University: Center on Education and the Workforce report, 13–14, 85, 86, 92, 98, 101, 104; University of Michigan compared with, 22, 23, 24

GI Bill, 75

Goodhart's law, 140–41

Goodman, Joshua, 24–26

grading standards, 114, 123–24, 128, 165n21

graduate degrees, 17–18, 104

graduation rates: artificially inflating, 31, 129; in college rankings, 2; college rankings compared with, 5, 21, 26, 27–28, 29, 31–32; differences in, 31–32; earnings and, 32, 48; financial aide and, 46–47; as indicator, 2; of lower-income students, 31, 32, 129; of racial minorities, 32, 44, 47, 129; selectivity and, 44–46, 151n31; services that improve, 46; spending per student and, 47–49; value-added, 15–16

Hanson, Andrew R., *48, 49*

Harvard University, 21, 25, 98–99

higher education: bureaucracies in, 135, 136, 139; health and well-being resulting from, 12, 19; metrics change, 134; Obama on value of, 11, 19; privatizing, 77–80, 82–83; social benefits of, 9, 19; upward mobility sought from, 120; value of, 8–9, 18–19, 81, 83; Veblen's criticisms of, 134–37; what is a good college, 33, 149n1. *See also* college (university) degrees (bachelor's degrees); college (university) rankings; cost of college; graduation rates; majors; public universities; return on investment (ROI); selectivity; spending per student; student debt

history majors, 37, *38,* 90, 92

honors colleges, 46

Hoover, Eric, 40–42

Hoxby, Caroline, 64, 162n6

"human capital," 112

humanities: classics, 135; class sizes in, 165n22; earnings in, 86, 88, 89, 105, *108,* 109–10; English majors, 98, 111; grade inflation in, *124*; history majors, 37, *38,* 90, 92; return on investment estimates and, 17, 18; student employment preferences and, 97; underrepresented minorities and lower-income students in, 120–22; Veblen on, 135. *See also* liberal arts